THE NEW
UNDERGROUND THEATRE

Edited by

ROBERT J. SCHROEDER, *comp.*

THE NEW UNDERGROUND THEATRE

A Bantam World Drama edition / published May 1968

PS
634
.S33

ACKNOWLEDGMENTS

PROMENADE. *Printed by permission of Maria Irene Fornes. Copyright © 1968 by Maria Irene Fornes.*

I'M REALLY HERE. *Printed by permission of Jean-Claude van Itallie. Copyright © 1966, 7 by Jean-Claude van Itallie. For information regarding professional use of the play, the author's agent should be contacted, Janet Roberts, London International, 65 East 55th Street, New York, N.Y., and for amateur rights information, Dramatist's Play Service, 440 Park Avenue South, New York, N.Y.*

THE GOLDEN SCREW *or* That's Your Thing, Baby. *Printed by permission of Thomas Sankey. Copyright © 1967 by Thomas Sankey. All rights reserved. Music: Reprinted by permission of Pronto Music Incorporated and Janet Day Music Company. Copyright © 1967 by Pronto Music Incorporated and Janet Day Music Company. All rights reserved.*

RED CROSS. *Reprinted by permission of the publishers, The Bobbs-Merrill Company, Inc. From* Five Plays *by Sam Shepard, copyright © 1967, by Sam Shepard.*

SAND. *Printed by permission of Murray Mednick. Copyright © 1967 by Murray Mednick. Caution: this play is fully protected by copyright. All inquiries concerning permission to perform part or all of this script in any way, including readings, in amateur or professional theatre, should be directed to Miss Carolyn Jenks, Authors' Representative, 191 Ninth Avenue, New York, N.Y. 10011.*

FRUIT SALAD. *Printed by permission of Grant Duay. Copyright © 1968 by Grant Duay. All inquiries should be addressed to the author c/o Bantam Books, Inc., 271 Madison Avenue, New York, N.Y. 10016.*

ISTANBUL. *Printed by permission of Rochelle Owens. Copyright © 1968 by Rochelle Owens.*

THE LIFE OF LADY GODIVA. *Printed by permission of Ronald Tavel. Copyright 1965 by Ronald Tavel. All rights reserved.*

Library of Congress Catalog Card Number: 68-19252

Published simultaneously in the United States and Canada

Bantam Books are published by Bantam Books, Inc., a subsidiary of Grosset & Dunlap, Inc. Its trade-mark, consisting of the words "Bantam Books" and the portrayal of a bantam, is registered in the United States Patent Office and in other countries. Marca Registrada. Bantam Books, Inc., 271 Madison Avenue, New York, N.Y. 10016.

CONTENTS

INTRODUCTION

The plays in this volume represent the theatrical expression of the anti-tradition and anti-Establishment revolution that shapes most of the output of the non-academic American artistic community of the 1960's.

American drama on Broadway evolves from the well-made play principles of Scribe and Hebbel, the social realism of Ibsen, Shaw and Chekhov, and the psychological probing of Strindberg and O'Neill. The underground theatre of New York and San Francisco takes the opposite tack. Its plays are spun out of fantasy and intuition. Their reality is that of unspoiled child-like insight. Their probing is more psychic than psychological.

The manner of acting and directing American plays on the commercial stage is based on the traditions of the English theatre and the inner truth focus of Stanislavski's "Method." The underground theatre defies all traditionalism and training. Its actors are provoked to an uninhibited and purposely uninformed naiveté.

The established American theatre often appears to think first of real estate and then of plays to perform in the buildings. Underground plays are presented in otherwise unused church lofts, coffee houses, cellars, empty lofts and store buildings. It is not unusual to find a playwright, a director and an acting troupe moving almost like the medieval strolling players, from loft to loft, and from neighborhood to neighborhood, constantly harried by city zoning officials and permit-checkers.

For the underground playwright as well as for the pop artist, the cultural traditions that have informed writers and artists since the Renaissance are no longer viable. The tradition of careful study of the works of the past and apprenticeship is given short shrift by the new dramatist.

Like their counterparts in the visual and aural arts,

these playwrights point to the technological, social changes that have taken place since Ibsen, Shaw and O'Neill, and insist that modern man's new environment requires a new artistic response. The new dramatist recognizes that we live in an era so unlike any preceding time that art can become art again only by an utter shedding of its constricting past and a complete rebirth.

The new theatre springs from a commitment to non-commitment, and a determined courting of indeterminacy that comprises quite as revolutionary an anti-doctrine as the post-Renaissance Western mind can conceive.

The plays included in this volume make up a representative sampling of the new underground theatre. They are selected from the several hundred underground plays that the editor has attended over the past several years.

Sam Shepard's *Red Cross* and Murray Mednick's *Sand* are prime examples of what might be called the underground's school of manic monologue. Their characters take turns in spinning intriguing whirls of imaginative fancy in obsessively incongruous circumstances. Forsaking dramatic confrontations, these plays induce a feeling of jarring disorientation like the wiggles and dazzles of op art. They instigate a heightened awareness of the bizarre, irrational reaches of human expression.

Murray Mednick is nihilistic philosophically as well as dramaturgically. His plays deny all existing principles, values or institutions.

Sam Shepard's plays are concerned with the celebration of innocence. Shepard asks his audience to shake off its preconceptions and stereotypic reactions. Like a New Testament preacher, he pleads for a recovery of innocence and a spiritual rebirth.

Ronald Tavel's *The Life of Lady Godiva*, Maria Irene Fornes' *Promenade* and Rochelle Owens' *Istanboul* comment on the sociological and psychological situation of twentieth century Americans in terms of movie-derived fantasy. Like many of the underground plays they satirize the story treatments, scenario patterns and clichés of the American movies of the thirties and forties. Like Andy Warhol's famous repetitive reproduction of Marilyn Monroe, these plays use the movies' familiar devices to explore, identify and emphasize those insights which the clichés normally obscure.

Maria Irene Fornes' forte is highly insightful whimsy. Ronald Tavel's plays mock the traditions of theology, philosophy and history. The staging of Tavel's work can best be pictured by imagining a Cecil B. De Mille technicolor extravaganza written, filmed and edited by a "high" crew expressly for private showings at stag-parties. Rochelle Owens' interest lies in the gap that separates man's pretended aspirations from his violent pack-animal impulses. While her plays cope with the same energies that captivated Strindberg and O'Neill, she presents her insights in a context of the bizarre and the incongruous.

Jean-Claude van Itallie's *I'm Really Here,* Grant Duay's *Fruit Salad* and Tom Sankey's *The Golden Screw* are examples of a third category of the new underground theatre. These plays eschew the manic hallucination of the Shepard-Mednick school and the broad generalities of the Tavel-Fornes-Owens genre. Instead Van Itallie, Duay and Sankey come to specific grips with recognizably American situations.

I'm Really Here is Jean-Claude van Itallie's fantasy portrait of the tragic end product of the American dream. Tom Sankey's *The Golden Screw* juxtaposes surrealistic musical commentary in a rock-and-roll vein with vaudeville-type black-out scenes. While its songs appear to be fragmented and unrelated, their cumulative effect gives a shocking sense of the America and the Americans of the 1960's. Grant Duay's *Fruit Salad* is a mixed-media presentation, devised by an artist who has worked most often in film. At first what goes on on the screen seems to have little relation to the simultaneous events on stage but then the play explodes into a searingly nihilistic statement about our kind of people in our kind of wars.

It is important to realize that the underground theatre is not likely to have evolved in its present form without a receptive audience. The underground theatre's strongholds are in Greenwich Village and San Francisco where a number of people actively dissociate themselves from the predominant American culture. They see the overt culture of the United States in the 1960's as a gigantic corporate complex of massive government and quasi-governmental agencies which breeds wars of "righteousness" that no one seems to start and no one knows how to end.

The underground theatre expresses its dissent from this society. It draws on an audience that wants to see art that is unlike "uptown" art; that wants to see movies that are its very own; and that wants its own theatre.

This audience brings to the underground playwright considerably more willingness to listen and to be aware than most audiences bring to the modern theatre. It seems fair to say that the average commercial audience sits down in a theatre, relaxes and says in effect to the playwright and to the actors, "Go on and entertain me— if you can." But generally speaking, the underground theatregoer asks the author and the players to challenge his imagination and his receptivity.

This is the basic reason why underground theatre "works" for the underground audience. For the new underground theatre emphatically does not do what Aristotle, Lessing, Racine, Hazlitt or Coleridge said that theatre is supposed to do. The new underground theatre does not arouse pity or awe. It does not educate or inspire or uplift its audiences. It is neither noble nor rhetorical. It does not become a temple of the passions. It is not philosophically contemplative. It does not seek to beguile with poetic subtlety or grandeur of language. It is not larger than life. It does not aspire to aesthetic beauty in any traditional sense.

Even Samuel Beckett (who in the context of underground theatre seems arriere-garde and bourgeois) has said that the playwright must, in order to be heard, insinuate his message into either the laugh or the tear. The new playwrights do not deign to such audience concessions.

However, for that audience that is willing to approach it sympathetically, lending it all possible receptivity and awareness, this new theatre makes available an unmediated perception that is probably without precedent in the theatre's long history. It intentionally sacrifices story-line,

suspense, naturalistic representation, characterization, ro-
mance, vicarious identification with a star, sympathy-
arousal, mirth-provocation (and even the courting of
audience "approval") for the stubbornly single-minded
purpose of triggering a radically deranged and psychically
liberating—or shall we say a "mind-blitzing" or even a
"mind-blowing"—beyond-the-rational insight into the human soul.

—R. J. Schroeder

New York City
July 1967

PROMENADE

Maria Irene Fornes

Playbill for Premiere Production

PROMENADE

by Maria Irene Fornes

Music by Al Carmines

Presented at Judson Poets' Theatre
(Judson Memorial Church, New York City)

Directed by Lawrence Kornfeld

CAST IN ORDER OF APPEARANCE

105	David Vaughn
106	George Bartenieff
JAILER	Michael Elias
MISS C.	Gretal Cummings
MISS F.	Crystal Field
MISS B.	Joan Fairlee
MR. T.	John Toland
MR. J.	Christopher Jones
MR. R.	Christopher Ross
SERVANT	Sheila Roy
MISS CAKE	Florence Tarlow
WAITER	Howard Roy

CHINAMAN ....Frank Emerson
WARDEN ....William Pardue
MOTHER ....Jerri Banks
PIANIST................................Al Carmines

Sets: Malcolm Spoooner
Costumes: Ellen Levene, Maria Irene Fornes
Lighting: Kathy Lewis

––––––––––

MARIA IRENE FORNES

Maria Irene Fornes was born in Cuba in 1930, and came to the United States in 1945. She began writing plays in 1961.

She is also a painter, and before becoming a playwright she spent several years in Europe concentrating on painting.

In addition to her other creative talents, Miss Fornes frequently designs and makes the costumes for Judson Poets' Theatre offerings.

She is a member of the writers' unit of the Actors Studio, and of The Open Theatre.

SCENE I

(The Cell. 105 and 106 dig and sing.)

105 *and* 106
> Dig, dig, dig
> A hole to be free.
> Dig a hole. Dig a hole.
> A hole to be free.

(The JAILER *enters. He is out of breath. He sits and dries his forehead.)*

JAILER.   It's been a hard day.

105 *and* 106.
> Dig, dig, dig.

JAILER.   Screwing all day.

105 *and* 106.
> A hole to be free.

JAILER.   Visiting days are hard working days. Screw, screw, nothing but screw.

105 *and* 106.
> Dig a hole. Dig a hole.
> A hole to be free.

JAILER.   34's wife, 48's daughter, and 108's widow.

105 *and* 106.
> Fly the coop.
> Break the wall.
> See the sun.

5

JAILER.   Well, better get back to the ladies. Just came up for some air . . . What are you two doing there?

105 *and* 106.
>   Dig a hole. Dig a hole.
>   A hole to be free.

JAILER.   Hm. You look like you're digging. Well, I'm going back to the widow. Better get in all the screwing I can before she finds out her old man's dead . . . So long, boys . . . Hm . . . You look like you're digging.

105 *and* 106.
>   Unacquainted with evil we are.
>   This shelter protects us from wrong.
>   To discover the appearance of sin
>   We must go where the dog takes a leak.

JAILER.   So long boys . . . By the way, if you want to get visitors just let me know. I can arrange it for you. (*Laughs loudly and walks away.*)

105 *and* 106.
>   The hole is dug.
>   Here we go.

(*105 and 106 disappear through the hole.*)

SCENE II

(*The Banquet. There are ladies and gentlemen in evening clothes around the table. The* SERVANT *sweeps. 105 and 106 enter. They put on top hats and tails. They sit at the table and eat.*)

MR. R.   Speech . . . Speech . . .

MR. S.   Let's play croquet . . .

MR. R.   Speeches and music . . .

MR. T.   Let's call Mr. Lipschitz . . .

MR. S.   No speeches . . . No speeches . . .

MR. R.   Let's have a song ...

MISS U.   Mr. T, was that you I saw in the corner of Fifth and Tenth?

MR. T.   Perhaps.

MISS U.   With Mrs. Schumann and her newly clipped poodle?

MR. T.   It couldn't have been me. Friday night I was out of town.

(They all laugh.)

MISS U.   And how did you know it was Friday night I saw you in the corner of Fifth?

MR. T.   Oh! Well, I must confess. The lady loves me.

MISS O.   She shows good taste.

(They all laugh.)

MR. S.   Then, introduce us. She'll surely fall for me.

(They all laugh.)

Let's have a song.

(105 and 106 stand, and get ready to sing.)

MISS I.   And who are these?

(105 and 106 realize they have been indiscreet and conceal themselves.)

MISS O.   They must be friends of Mr. S.

(They all laugh.)

MISS I.   You hit it on the nail.

MR. S.   If I am sometimes in the company of this and that, it's only because I like to study life.

(They all laugh.)

MR. R.   The song. The song. Let's have a song. *(He points to MISS O.)*

MISS O. The song can wait. (*She smiles coyly and sings.*)

> You were there when I was not.
> I was there when you were not.
> Don't love me, sweetheart
> Or I might stop loving you.
> Unrequited love.
> Unrequited love.

MISS I.

> Passionate lips are sweet.
> But, oh, how much sweeter
> Are lips that refuse.
> Don't love me, sweetheart
> Or I might stop loving you.

MISS U.

> Inviting lips
> Alluring lips
> Which shape the word no
> No no no no no no.
> Don't love me, sweetheart
> Or I might stop loving you.

MR. R.

> You know nothing of life.
> You know nothing of love
> Till you have tasted
> Of unrequited love.
> Don't love me, sweetheart
> Or I might stop loving you.

ALL.

> Unrequited love.
> Unrequited love.
> There is no love.
> Like unrequited love.

MISS I. Oh! We sung that well.

MR. S. He who scrubs the pot finds it most shiny.

MR. R. And he who soils it turns up his nose.

MISS I. Touché!

MISS U. What a marvellous mind!

MR. R. Just frank.

SERVANT (*mimicking*). Just frank.

(*They all look at her with surprise. A giant cardboard cake is brought in.*)

MR. S. Look! It's time for dessert.

LADIES.

> Don't eat it.
> Don't eat it.
> Wait until midnight.

GENTLEMEN.

> . Put it on the table.
> Put it on the table.

MISS U. Phooey . . . It smells of garlic.

MR. T.

> It's not to be eaten.
> It's not to be eaten.

(*The top of the cake opens and* MISS CAKE *steps out. The* GENTLEMEN *carry her to the table.*)

LADIES.

> Don't eat her.
> Don't eat her.
> Wait until midnight.

GENTLEMEN.

> Put her on the table.
> Put her on the table.

LADIES.

> She's not to be eaten.
> She's not to be eaten.

MISS I. What is she for?

MR. R. To look at.

MR. S.   And to touch.

MR. R.   Only to touch.

MR. S.   And to look at.

MISS I.   May the ladies touch, too?

MR. R.   No, not the ladies, only the gentlemen.

MISS I (*starting to take off her clothes*).   I want to be naked too.

MR. R.

> Only one.
> Only one
> Naked lady.

MISS I (*undressing*).

> Two ... Two.
> I want to be naked too.

MR. R.

> Only one.
> Only one
> Naked lady.
> All right, two
> Two naked ladies.

MISS I.

> Thank you.
> Thank you, sir.

GENTLEMEN.

> Only two.
> Only two
> Naked ladies.

MISS U (*undressing*).

> Three ... Three.
> I want to be naked too.

GENTLEMEN.

> Only two.
> Only two
> Naked ladies.

                All right, three
                Three naked ladies.

MISS U.

                Thank you.
                Thank you, sir.

GENTLEMEN.

                Only three.
                Only three
                Naked ladies.

MISS O (*undressing*).

                Four . . . Four.
                I want to be naked too.

GENTLEMEN.

                Only three.
                Only three
                Naked ladies.
                All right, four
                Four naked ladies.

MISS O.

                Thank you.
                Thank you, sir.

ALL.

                Only four.
                Only four
                Naked ladies.
                Four . . . Four
                Four naked ladies.

LADIES.

                Thank you.
                Thank you, sir.

(*The* LADIES *put their dresses back on.*)

MISS I.   Mademoiselle, comment vous appelez-vous?

MISS CAKE.   Moi, je m'appelle, La Rose de Shanghai.

MISS U.   Est-ce que vous êtes français?

MISS CAKE. Pas aujourd 'hui.
Let the fruit ripen on the tree
For if not the meat will harden.
I'm the peach of the west.
Chicken is he who does not love me.

I come from a country named America.

MR. R. You do?

MISS CAKE. I do.
Chicken is he who does not love me.
For there's more to the cake than the icing
A morsel I'm not, I'm a feast.
And this not every man knows.
Remember all the times
You thought you got a bargain?

MISS O. I do.

MISS CAKE.
And it cost you more than it was worth?

MISS U. Aha!

MISS CAKE.
That's what we're here for.
To learn one thing or another.
For on art alone one cannot live.
Chicken is he who does not love me.

Tell me you adore me, and I'll let you go.

ALL.
We adore you.

MISS CAKE.
I'm the peach of the west, you know.
And a bit of a rebel, just a bit.
And chicken is he, chicken are you all.
I'm not a morsel, I'm a feast.
I'm not a morsel, I'm a feast.
I'm not a morsel, I'm a feast.

(*Through the following scene 105 and 106 empty
the pockets of the guests. They steal silverware*

and candlesticks. They put the loot in sacks they carry with them.)

MR. R. A toast . . . A toast . . .

MR. S. To the ladies . . . To the ladies . . .

ALL.

> Only four.
> Only four
> Naked ladies.
> Four . . . Four . . .
> Four naked ladies.

LADIES.

> Thank you.
> Thank you, sir.

(The JAILER *enters.)*

JAILER. Everybody's under arrest.

MR. S. No we're not. We're having a banquet.

JAILER. I want to be naked too. *(He starts taking off his clothes.)*

MR. T. Not the gentlemen . . . The gentlemen in full dress.

JAILER. I'll keep my underwear on.

MR. S. The gentlemen in full dress. Don't take your clothes off.

(The JAILER *takes off his clothes. He wears long underwear.)*

JAILER. In this country we have the best crime.

MR. S. Yes, yes. We have the best of everything.

(The banquet GUESTS *become drowsy.* 105 *and* 106 *sing.)*

105 *and* 106.

> Can you bear this bliss?

No . . .
Can you bear this bliss?
Yes . . .

Eating is a blessing.
Money is a joy.
Drinking is a pleasure
And riches a delight.

We've come to one conclusion
That's readily discerned;
A lot of satisfaction
Does away with discontent.

Doesn't it?
A lot of satisfaction
Produces happiness.
And the source of satisfaction
Is wealth.
Isn't it?
All that man possesses
Displaces discontent.

SERVANT.   What? What? What? What? What?

105 *and* 106.

Diamond and cakes
Macaroons and furs
Dispel discontent.
Chandeliers and wine
Porcelain and lace
Efface discontent.

Silverware and hats
Embroideries and salt
Flowerpots and yachts
Cinnamon and bells
And awnings
And cushions
And satins
And rings
And castles
And
And things

> Things
> Things
> Things
> Be content!

SERVANT (*as she sweeps*). Riches made them dumb. Yes, riches made them dumb.

> (*105 and 106 look at the* GUESTS. *They look at the* SERVANT. *She nods.*)

105 *and* 106. It's not worth it, then.

SERVANT. It's worth it.

105 *and* 106. Are you rich?

> (*The* SERVANT *shakes her head.*)

Are you smart?

> (*The* SERVANT *shrugs her shoulders.*)

You might as well be rich, then.

SERVANT. I'm trying.

105 *and* 106. How?

> (*She shows them the broom. They give her a diamond ring and a wallet from their sacks.*)

JAILER (*remembering*).
> Dig, dig, dig
> A hole to be free.

MR. S. What kind of stupid song is that?

JAILER. They dug a hole. That's how they got out. They were singing;
> Dig, dig, dig
> A hole to be free.

And they were digging a hole. I have to tell the warden.

> (*105 and 106 run toward the door. The* JAILER *runs also. 105, 106 and the* JAILER *bump against each other. The* JAILER *doesn't recognize them.*)

JAILER. Aprés vous.

105 *and* 106. Aprés vous.

JAILER. Pas du tout.

105 *and* 106. Je vous en prie.

JAILER. Mon plaisir.

105 *and* 106. Le nôtre.

JAILER. Permettez!

105 *and* 106. Notre plaisir.

JAILER. Le mien.

105 *and* 106. À votre service.

JAILER. L'âge avant la beauté.

(MR. T *kicks the* JAILER *out of the door.* 105, 106 *and the* SERVANT *follow.*)

MR. T. Let's play croquet!

ALL (*as they exit*).
> Can you bear this bliss?
> No . . .
> Can you bear this bliss?
> Yes . . .
> Eating is a blessing.
> Money is a joy.
> Drinking is a pleasure
> And riches a delight.

SCENE III

(*The Park. The* MOTHER *enters. She looks for her babies.*)

MOTHER.
> Have you seen my babies?
> I've been looking for them

For years.
And I can't find them.

Have you seen them?
Have you seen them?
Have you seen them?

(*The* MOTHER *exits.* 105's, 106's *and the* SERVANT's *heads appear from behind the bushes.* 105 *and* 106 *bury their sacks. They enjoy the fresh air, and sit on the grass.*)

105. Did you really like that party?

106. Yes . . . I liked it . . .

105. I liked it too . . .

106. You did?

105. Yes . . .

(*There is the sound of traffic.*)

You know?

106. What?

105. To discover what everyone has always known is not important.

106. No, it isn't.

105. However . . .

106. What?

SERVANT. *What?*

105. I've just discovered what life is all about.

106. You have?

(105 *nods.*)

SERVANT. What is it about?

105.
　　　　To walk down the street

With a mean look in my face.
A cigarette in my right hand
A toothpick in the left.
To alternate between the cigarette
And the toothpick
Ah! That's life.

(105, 106 *and the* SERVANT *repeat the first stanza.*)

105 *and* 106.
Yes, I've learned from life.
Every day I've learned some more.
Every blow has been of use.
Every joy has been a lesson.
What surprises me
Is that life
Has not learned from me.

105 (*to the audience*). Why? . . . Well . . . That
would be hard to explain . . . If I could give you a kiss
you'd understand. (*Blows a kiss to the audience.*) You
still don't understand?

106. Wait. (*Blows a kiss to the audience.*)

105 *and* 106. No? . . .
Well, then,
Because I'm placid as a cow
As lucid as glass
As frank as a bold head
As faithful as a dog.

(*They exit.*)

SCENE IV

(*The Street. There is the sound of a car and a
crash. Then the sound of the car again. A* MAN *lies
wounded on the ground.* 105, 106 *and the* SERVANT
enter. 105 *and* 106 *look the* WOUNDED MAN *over,
empty his pockets, take his clothes off, and put
the loot in their sacks. They start walking away.*)

WOUNDED MAN.   Oh. Oh.

> (105 *and* 106 *walk back and watch the* WOUNDED
> MAN. *The* DRIVER *enters.*)

DRIVER.   I came back.

WOUNDED MAN.   Oh. Oh.

DRIVER.   To the scene of the crime.

WOUNDED MAN.   Oh. Oh.

DRIVER.   I'm a hit and run driver.

WOUNDED MAN.   Oh. Oh.

DRIVER.   I'll kill myself if you die.

WOUNDED MAN.   Oh. Oh. I'm cold.

> (*The* JAILER *enters.*)

JAILER.   Have you seen two prisoners escaped from
the penitentiary? One tall and the other just a little
taller?

> (105 *and* 106 *lie as if wounded.*)

They have black hair and wear prisoners' uniforms with
the numbers 105 and 106 on the front and on the back
of their jackets.

> (105 *and* 106 *take off their jackets and put them
> on the* WOUNDED MAN. *One number is visible on
> his chest and the other on his back.*)

WOUNDED MAN.
> Thank you. Thank you.
> You're so nice. You're so nice.
> Thank you. Thank you.
> You're so nice. You're so nice.
> Thank you.

JAILER (*pointing to the* WOUNDED MAN).   That's one
of them! Get up 105. (*Kicks the* WOUNDED MAN *over.
The number* 106 *is visible on his back.*) There's the
other. Get up 106. That's them all right. Get up.

DRIVER.   Leave him alone. You're kicking the wounded man.

JAILER.   What do you mean? That's 105 and 106.

DRIVER.   Does that look like two people to you? That's the wounded man.

(105 *and* 106 *begin to shiver.*)

WOUNDED MAN.   My friends are cold, too. Someone must have stolen their clothes.

DRIVER.   I'll take the clothes off my back to give to your friends. If you die I'd kill myself.

(*The* DRIVER *gives his jacket and vest to* 105 *and* 106. *He shivers. The* WOUNDED MAN *gives one of the prisoners' jackets to the* DRIVER.)

WOUNDED MAN.   I have enough for two.

JAILER.   Which reminds me of this little woman I used to have. She used to change her clothes all the time. That was the only thing I liked about her . . . Hey! There you are, 105 and 106. Don't tell me you're just one. I see you as plain as day. One and two. I can count. Don't tell me I can't count. (*Takes the* DRIVER *and the* WOUNDED MAN *by the collar and walks away with them.*)

SERVANT.

> Neither probe nor ignore
> That the clothes make the man.
> Isn't it true that costumes
> Change the course of life?

ALL.

> Who can marry a gigolo?
> Can you?
> Can you?
> I can't.
>
> Who can love a businessman?
> Can you?

> Can you?
> I can't.
>
> Who can pity a cop?
> Who can reason with a clown?
> Who can dance with a priest?
> Can you?
> Can you?
> I can't.
>
> You see, a costume
> Can change your life.
> Be one and all.
> Be each and all.
> Transvest
> Impersonate
> 'Cause costumes
> Change the course
> Of life.

(*The* JAILER *re-enters wearing the prisoners' jackets.*)

JAILER. I'm taking these two prisoners back to jail.
(*Shrugs his shoulders and exits.*)

ALL.

> Who can argue with a jailer?
> Can you?
> Can you?
> I can't.
>
> Be one and all.
> Be each and all.
> Transvest
> Impersonate
> 'Cause costumes
> Change the course
> Of life.

(*The* JAILER *comes running in.* 105, 106 *and the*
SERVANT *run off stage. The* JAILER *follows.*)

JAILER. You tricked me, you singing buggers.

SCENE V

(The Park. 105 and 106 sit on a bench. They knit each end of a single scarf. The MOTHER *enters.)*

MOTHER. I've lost my babies. I've been looking for them for years and I can't find them. Have you seen them?

106. No.

MOTHER. You haven't seen my babies, have you? They aren't very pretty but they have dark eyes.

105. No.

MOTHER. I lost my babies right here. Have you seen them?

105 *and* 106. No.

(The MOTHER *looks closely at 105 and 106.)*

MOTHER. No . . . My babies were pretty. These are not my babies.

(She looks again. 105 and 106 try to look pretty.) No. These are big, ugly and old. Mine were this big. *(She indicates the size of an infant.)* And pretty. Good bye.

105 *and* 106. Good bye.

(The MOTHER *walks to the bushes and hides there. She observes 105 and 106.)*

> It's to age
> That we owe
> What we are.
> In fact we're grateful
> For the passing of time.
> It's only fitting
> We should be grateful

For the passing of time.
'Cause
Without growth
We'd not be
What we are.

MOTHER (*from the bushes*).
    What are you?

(*They pose for her. They point to themselves from head to toe. They do a turn. They do a tap step.*)

105 *and* 106.
    We are
    All
    That we are.
    From head to toe.

Once it's thoroughly thought through
We should realize
It's only appropriate
We should be attracted
To the passing of time.
Attracted to the passing of time.
'Cause it's to age
That we owe what we are.
And without it
We'd not be
What we are.

MOTHER (*from the bushes*). It's distressing to get old.

105 *and* 106. Woe . . . Woe . . . Woe . . . Woe . . .

MOTHER (*coming out of the bushes*). It's not that bad.

(*The MOTHER, 105 and 106 repeat the last stanza. The JAILER enters.*)

JAILER. I saw you. Running won't do you any good. (*Runs past them and off the stage.*)

(*The SERVANT enters with a roast and champagne. They sit down to eat. The JAILER re-enters.*)

You tricked me. You didn't run.

> (105 *and* 106 *run off stage. The* JAILER *follows. The
> banquet* GUESTS *walk through.* 105 *and* 106 *are
> among them.*)

MR. R.   Who's first at croquet?

MISS U.   Let's all be first.

MISS O.   Phooey. Let's not play croquet.

MR. R.   Speech, please, a little speech.

MR. T.   I just called Mr. Lipschitz.

MR. S.   Let's go to the warden's party. He's a very
amusing fellow.

> (105 *and* 106, *the* MOTHER *and the* SERVANT *follow
> the banquet* GUESTS *arm in arm.*)

106.   Shall we have a little speech?

105.   Yes. Yes. Let's all speak first.

ALL.   To the warden's. To the warden's.

> (105 *and* 106 *take a few steps back. They discuss
> whether they should go to the warden's.* MISS I
> *takes* MR. T *by the hand, they take a few steps
> back.*)

MISS I.   Let us be irrational.

> (MR. T *walks away.*)

(*Opening her arms toward* 105 *and* 106.) Let's you and
me embrace.

> (105 *and* 106 *are confused as to which one she
> means. They bump against each other, bow to
> each other, offer the way to the other. They finally
> get to her with open arms.*)

The moment has passed.

> You have, perhaps, made me feel something

But the moment has passed.
And what is done cannot be undone.
Once a moment passes, it never comes again.

I once had a man who loved me well.
His mouth was smaller than his eye.
But I loved him just the same.
Yes, I loved him just the same.

He said he would kill for me.
And I said like for instance whom?
And he said like for instance you
Like for instance you.

Sometimes it hurts more than others.
Sometimes it hurts less.
Sometimes it's just the same.
Sometimes it's really just the same.

But never mind that.
No never mind that.
God gave understanding just to confuse us.
And it's always the same, anyway.
It's always the same, anyway.

If it's in your path to hurt me,
By all means do.
But, I beg you don't go out of your way.
Don't go out of your way to do so.

You don't know what to make of me.
But I know what to make of you.
I've nothing to lose
Or not much, anyway.
But never nimd that.
God gave understanding just to confuse us.
And it's always the same, anyway.

You have, perhaps, made me feel something
But the moment has passed.
And what is done cannot be undone.
Once a moment passes, it never comes again.

(*She exits.*)

SCENE VI

(*The Warden's Living Room. The* WARDEN *sits on a high chair. A stethoscope hangs from his neck. The* JAILER *and* MISS CAKE *stand by his side. The rest enter in the order they left the previous scene.*)

WARDEN. Welcome . . . Welcome . . . I am about to entertain. Whoever is not amused will be sent to the common cell.

JAILER. Hear. Hear. The show is about to start.

WARDEN. Has any of you ever heard the story of the rabbit and the turtle?

ALL. Yes.

WARDEN. You see, it goes like this: There was once a rabbit who said to the turtle, "Run fast. Run fast, or I'll win the race." "I'll run slowly," said the turtle, "and win the race." "If that is the case, I'll take a rest," said the rabbit. "Why?" said the turtle. "To give you an advantage," said the rabbit. "Who are you to give me advantages," said the turtle. And so on . . . and so on . . . and so on . . . Whoever doesn't laugh will be sent to the common cell.

(*They all laugh.*)

Good. Now the party's over. Let me see what time it is. (*Looking at his watch.*) Too late! Everybody's under arrest for keeping me up so late. Wait, you've been reprieved. My watch stopped. It must be earlier than I thought. Or later. Amuse yourselves. I give the best parties in town. I don't? Who said that? I must be hearing things again. No one would dare say I don't give the best parties in town. I must be crazy. Now, who has some mighty good entertainment?

(MR. R, MR. S, *and* MR. T *walk to the center in a vaudevillian manner.*)

MR. R.   This is my son. (*Apologetically.*) He needs a haircut.

MR. S.   What he needs is a new face.

(MR. R, MR. S *and* MR. T *laugh heartily.*)

WARDEN.   Pretty dull. Pretty dull. I have seen better entertainment than that. Like for instance. (*Sings and bends his fingers.*)

Whenever my fingers went like this.
I said: Hell, my fingers always go like that.
Until one day somebody said to me:
How original it is that your fingers go like that.

Since then, every time my fingers go like this.
I say: Look at my fingers go like that.
How original it is that my fingers go like this.
One of these days I'll sell them.

That's good entertainment. No one can top that. Who's next?

(MR. T *takes out a song sheet. He gets the key from the piano and sings.*)

MR. T.

It is true I told you I would love you
And I never did.
But remember I'm forgetful,
Little fool.
Longings are like vapor.
They come as they go.
And remember little fool.
I'm forgetful.

Both, my wife's and my mistress' name is Kate.
One day, while I made love to Kate, my wife,
I thought of my sweet mistress Kate.
In a moment of passion and confusion,
I said, Kate, dear Kate, oh, Kate.
My wife, hearing me say my mistress' name.
Said harsh words to me. And put me on the street.
Is that fair, I ask you, is that fair.

It is true I told you I would love you,
And I never did.
But remember I'm forgetful,
Little fool.
Longings are like vapor.
They come as they go.
And remember little fool.
I'm forgetful.

(*The* GUESTS *applaud.*)

WARDEN. No good. No good. That's common and ordinary. I'm a poet and a scholar. Let's hear some poetry.

105. Miss Cake.

MISS CAKE. Yes, Mr. 105.

106. What do you aim at in your work?

MISS CAKE. Magic.

105. Do you always achieve it?

MISS CAKE. Yes. Once in a while.

106. You don't mean always, then.

MISS CAKE. Yes, I do.

105. Explain.

MISS CAKE. In mathematical terms, if the impossible is ever achieved, it becomes always. That is how eternity is conceived.

(MISS CAKE *takes a bow. The rest applaud.*)

WARDEN. That makes sense. But that's not poetry. That's science. Go back to your cake. Now this is poetry.

A petunia is a flower like a begonia.
You fry begonia like you fry sausage.
Sausage and battery is a crime.
Monkeys crime trees.
Tree is a crowd.
The cock crowd and made a noise.

You have a noise on your face, also two eyes.
The opposite of eyes is nays.
A horse nays and has a colt.
You go to bed with a colt.
And wake up with double petunia.

Whoever doesn't laugh will be sent to the common cell.

(*The* WARDEN *uses his stethoscope to make sure that everyone is laughing. They all laugh except* 105 *and* 106. *He signals the* JAILER *to take them away. As the* JAILER *walks off with* 105 *and* 106 *the* MOTHER *climbs the staircase and sings.*)

MOTHER.

Does anyone understand a mother's love?
Except a mother?
Does a father understand a mother's love?
Except a good father?
Does anyone understand a mother's love?
Except a son, or a grandfather, or an uncle?

ALL.

Everyone.

MOTHER (*recitative*).

Then do you know that one autumn afternoon
My children disappeared and that that very
Autumn afternoon my life ended?

(*The* JAILER *returns holding two* MEN *wearing cooks' outfits.*)

WARDEN. I thought I told you to take those two prisoners away.

MOTHER. Don't take my children away.

JAILER. I went the wrong way. That's the kitchen.

WARDEN. March on.

MOTHER. I must kill myself.

(*The* MOTHER *jumps from the staircase.* 105 *and* 106 *enter in time to catch her.*)

WARDEN.   Marvellous. Marvellous. That's mighty good entertainment. Do it again.

(*The* MOTHER *goes up the steps and jumps again.* 105 *and* 106 *catch her.*)

Now the party is over. Let me see what time it is. Too late! Everybody's under arrest for keeping me up so late.

(*The* JAILER *guides everyone out.*)

Good night. Marvellous . . . Marvellous entertainment.

SCENE VII

(*The Cell is empty. There is the sound of voices. All except the* WARDEN *enter.*)

JAILER.   The ladies are to come with me to the next cell, one at a time. It's too crowded here.

MR. S.   I'm tired of this party. I want to go home.

MR. R.   Let's go home.

MR. T.   Let's go home. Let's not start acting as if we're all criminals.

JAILER.   You can't go away. You're under arrest.

MR. S.   No, we're not.

JAILER.   Have some respect.

(*All except the* MOTHER, *the* JAILER, 105 *and* 106 *exit through the hole. The* JAILER *exits through the door and locks it.*)

MOTHER.   Did you have a good time, my children?

105 *and* 106.   Yes.

MOTHER.   Did you find evil?

105 *and* 106.   No.

MOTHER. Good night, then. Sleep well. You'll find it some other time.

105 *and* 106. Good night.

(*The* MOTHER *rocks them to sleep.*)

MOTHER.

> I saw a man lying on the street.
> Asleep and drunk.
> He had not washed his face.
> He held his coat closed with a safety pin.
> And I thought. And I thought:
> Thank God I'm better than he is.
> Yes, thank God, I'm better than he.
>
> I have to live with my own truth.
> I have to live with it.
> You live with your own truth.
> I cannot live with it.
> I have to live with my own truth.
> Whether you like it or not.
> Whether you like it or not.
>
> There are many poor people in the world.
> Whether you like it or not.
> There are many poor people in the world.
> But I'm not one of them.
> I'm not one of them.
> Someone's been stealing my apples.
> But I'm not one of them.
> I'm not one of them.
>
> I know everything.
> Half of it I really know.
> The rest I make up.
> The rest I make up.
> Some things I'm sure of.
> Of other things I'm too sure.
> And of others I'm not sure at all.
> People believe everything they hear
> Not what they see. Not what they see.
> People believe everything they hear.
> But me, I see everything.

Yes I see everything.

The saddest day of my life was the day.
I pitied a despicable man.
And I've been sad ever since.
Yes, I've been sad ever since.
I'd like to go where a human being
Is not a strange thing.
Is not a strange thing.
When I go no one will water my plants.
When I go no one will water my plants.
No one . . . No one . . . No one . . .

Yes, my children, you'll find evil . . . some other time
. . . Good night. (*She exits.*)

105 *and* 106.   Good night.

All is well in the city.
People do what they want.
They can go to the park.
They can sleep all they want.
And for those who have no cake,
There's plenty of bread.

(*Curtain.*)

I'M REALLY HERE

Jean-Claude van Itallie

Playbill for Premiere Production

I'M REALLY HERE
by Jean-Claude van Itallie

Presented at The Open Theatre
(Sheridan Square Playhouse, New York City)

Directed by Sydney Schubert Walter

(Editor's note: At the time of this production it was the policy of The Open Theatre company to alternate players, and not to list individual players with roles in their programs.)

THE COMPANY OF PLAYERS ON THE NIGHT OF THE PREMIERE

Joyce Aaron
James Barbosa
Valerie Belden
Isabelle Blau
Paul Boesing
Pat Donegan
Ron Faber
Sharon Gans
Marcia Kurtz
Gerome Ragni
David Spielberg
Barbara Vann
Sidney Schubert Walter
Lee Worley

Production assistants: Rhea Gaisner, Richard Orzel

JEAN-CLAUDE VAN ITALLIE

"I was born in Brussels, Belgium on May 25, 1936. My parents were Belgian. In May of 1940 the Germans invaded Belgium and my family fled through France, Spain, Portugal, arriving finally, aboard a Japanese boat (we weren't yet at war with them) in the United States. The day the Germans arrived in Brussels and we could hear the bombing I asked Mother what the noise was, and she replied it was the workmen working on a garage next door. I was raised in Great Neck, Long Island. I went to school there until my senior year of high school, when I went to Deerfield Academy in Massachusetts. I think the American suburbs are a lousy place to raise a child—the illusion of eternal safety and universal happiness is pernicious.

"I spent all my summers, after the age of eleven, in Europe, mostly in Belgium. After Deerfield which I did not like I went to Harvard, which I liked and toward which I feel still some attachment. I left Harvard for half of my sophomore year, going away, sophomorically, to 'suffer' as a car-hop in Washington, D.C. and then as a loafer in Paris. I graduated from Harvard in 1958, having spent most of my senior year directing plays. I moved to Greenwich Village after that, and have lived there in various apartments ever since, doing various jobs, mostly freelance—in the last two or three years they have been mostly writing TV public affairs scripts for the networks.

"In 1963, Dec. 22, my play *War* was presented at the Village South Theatre, and just about the same time I joined The Open Theatre. I had been writing before that, but never had the opportunity to see anything produced because it was too 'way out,' what I was writing. The scene has changed now, and off-off-Broadway has opened up to any writer who would find himself in the same position. I had plays presented here and there (Atlanta, Minneapolis, La Mama, Cino, Open Theatre, etc.) but my first commercial production was *America Hurrah* which opened in Nov. 1966. It's now being done in San Francisco and London, and I've translated it into French for a Belgian and a French production, and it's been sold to Scandinavia, Germany, Italy, etc. I spend as much time as possible on a farm I have in Massachusetts. I hope some of this is useful. This is the end of the page."

(The play is done by the actors as if it were a movie. When the individual actors are not, for a moment or two, "on camera," their expression is deadpan and bored. They are "on" for their "bits." Often DORIS *will make a tried-and-true facial expression especially for the camera, turning her face into a "cute" mask or a "hurt" mask, etc. She often addresses the camera instead of another actor. The actors always know exactly where the camera is at a given moment, whether the moment is a closeup, a two-shot, a helicopter shot, panning, etc.*

At the end of the play it is as if the cameras were locked in place. DORIS *could not get out of this movie now if she wanted to.)*

(A busload of American tourists (this can be done with a few chairs.) ROSSANO *holds a microphone in his hand. When the curtain opens the actors are relaxed in posture, inattentive. A moment later the light comes up pink, the Parisian-type music starts playing, and the actors, especially* DORIS, *express typical total delight and charm at the sights they see out the bus windows.*

DORIS *is getting her first "gander" at "that lady-known-as-Paris." She's thrilled of course, but knows better than to show it. With* ROSSANO *as a tour conductor, what twenty-six-year-old spinster with her head in the stars could keep her feet on the ground?)*

ROSSANO *(with a romantic accent)*. And on your left, ladies and gentlemen, is the Eiffel Tower.

DORIS. The Eiffel Tower! It's really here. I'm really there. Oh, pinch yourself, Doris, pinch yourself.

ROSSANO. We are now driving down the Champs Elysées. And before I drop you back at the cafe, I want you to know that I have never before had the pleasure of conducting such a lovely group of Americans before, never.

> (*They laugh and applaud him.* DORIS *knows he was staring right at her. The bus stops and the others get out.*)

ROSSANO. Welcome to Paris and, as they say in your own country, don't do anything I would not do.

> (DORIS *is the last one on the bus, being delayed pulling on her clear plastic booties and tying a kerchief around her head.*)

DORIS. You speak English very well.

ROSSANO. Thank you infinitely.

DORIS. Who taught you?

ROSSANO. A young American lady. An intimate friend.

DORIS. Oh. I suppose you meet many young American ladies in your line of work?

ROSSANO. Oh yes, many, many.

DORIS (*angrily pulling on her second booty*). I *see.*

ROSSANO. But never have I met so pretty a one as you.

DORIS (*relenting*). Oh no? Really? You know I bet you say that to all of them.

ROSSANO (*very hurt*). How unkind you are.

DORIS (*sorry she has wounded him*). Oh . . . I didn't mean to be. I'm sorry. I didn't mean to be uncharitable. Will you forgive me?

ROSSANO. Only if you will consent to my walking you back to your hotel.

DORIS. To my hotel? Consent? Well, I guess there can't be any real harm in it, can there? And it is Paris after all . . .

ROSSANO. Yes, yes it is Paris and you are young and it is spring and so let yourself go. Consent.

DORIS (*throwing caution to the winds*). All right. Alrighty okay. I consent. *Walk* me back to my hotel.

ROSSANO. That's the spirit.

DORIS. Here goes nothing. Keep your fingers crossed. Ready or not here I go.

(They step off the bus.)

ROSSANO.   Here you are in gay Paris.

DORIS.   Here I am. Wheeeeeee. Wheeeeee. Pareeeeee-eeeeee.

ROSSANO.   Already you are French. Oui, oui, Paris, it means yes, yes to Paris.

DORIS.   Alors then, oui, oui, Paris!

(Here they break into a song and softshoe number. Parisians going about their picturesque business on the streets and in the cafes are charmed with the blonde American mademoiselle so obviously enchanted with their city. They sit for a moment at a cafe where a waitress immediately brings them something with which they toast each other. He buys her some violets from an old lady. They pass an artist wearing a beret and she takes the paintbrush from him and puts the last perfect finishing touches on the canvas leaving the artist smiling broadly through clenched teeth.)

DORIS.   Oh. Oh my. Let me catch up with myself. I'm all winded. I'm tuckered. Plum. Mr. Brassy, I'm plum tuckered. *(She laughs.)*

ROSSANO.   How fresh you are. You are the spirit of spring. This is your hotel, no?

DORIS.   No. I mean yes. Yes it is.

ROSSANO.   Will you ask me up?

DORIS.   No! Up? *(She gulps.)*

ROSSANO.   Yes.

DORIS.   But I have a tiny room. There's only one chair in it. Where would you sit?

ROSSANO.   Is there no bed?

DORIS.   Bed? You want to sit on my *bed?*

ROSSANO.   But why not?

DORIS *(indignant).* Why not?! *(Now she has pity on his ignorance.)* Oh, Rossano. *(She speaks very kindly, as if to a small child.)* I don't want to sound superior because I'm from America but, you see, you have your little tribal customs—and I'm sure I don't want to know anything about them—but for an American woman, well, things are very different. I'm from the USA, Rossano. I'm not one of your *native* girls.

ROSSANO. But here in the Ancient World we have a wise old saying which goes—now repeat after me—when in Paris—

DORIS (*she closes her eyes and repeats after him until she realizes the implications of what she's saying*). When in Paris—

ROSSANO. Do as the Parisians.

DORIS. Do as the—oh, Rossano, I couldn't.

ROSSANO. But why not? You are young and it is spring and so let yourself go! Just say oui, oui Paris.

DORIS (*very sorry for him*). I'm sorry. I can't oui oui. Not to that. A girl has her limits, Rossano.

ROSSANO. Ah well, c'est la vie. This then is Goodbye. Arivederci. (*He kisses her hand.*) Au revoir, Miss Prettyasabutton.

DORIS. Oh. Au revoir, Mr. Brassy. You have made Paris . . . Paris for me.

(*She watches him leave. She is in a daze as she enters the hotel and goes into the elevator. The wise old elevator man knows.*

The elevator gate, elevator, room door, etc. can all be pantomined.)

DORIS. Two, please.

ELEVATOR MAN. Did you have a good afternoon, Miss Prettyasabutton?

DORIS. Dreamy. Just dreamy.

ELEVATOR MAN. I was sure of it. (*He lets her out.*) Let me open the door for you. Love makes you very helpless, doesn't it?

DORIS (*snapping indignantly out of it*). *Love?* Who said anything about love?

ELEVATOR MAN (*returning to elevator*). You can't fool a Parisian. I hope you will be very happy. Goodnight.

DORIS. Well! Really! (*She slams her door and then*

looks in the mirror.) Well, I must admit I do look a little like a hophead with that nutty grin on my funny little face and those goopy stars in my peepers. Why I'm like a crazy schoolgirl waiting for a bus. But what a silly I am. He's gone. I'll probably never see him again. Oh, Rossano. No. (*She stops herself from crying.*) Why, I just met the man today. Doris, you're such an ass. Now get a good firm grip on yourself. (*She marches about the room in sensible fashion, getting a "grip on herself."*) You're going to wash that man right out of your hair. You're going to run a hot bath and put some curlers in and wash your undies and be sensible. (*Suddenly she stops in her tracks, overcome with romantic memory.*) Oh, but he's so romantically inclined. (*She walks to the balcony, throws open the French doors, and looks out over the Seine.*) He's out there somewhere. Somewhere in Paris.

> (*Beneath the balcony someone is whistling softly. She hums along without thinking and then, in stages, it occurs to her that it could be, it might be, Rossano. She hums half a phrase of the song. He finishes the phrase, whistling. She knows it's him.*)

DORIS (*calling down to him*). Oh. Oh Rossano. Rossano, it's you.

ROSSANO (*calling up to her*). Doris, I couldn't leave.

DORIS (*shouting*). Oh, Rossano.

> (*She swoons, falls from the balcony, but fortunately he catches her deftly.*)

Oh, Rossano.

> (*Having landed in his arms she faints. After an instant there is a blackout. When the lights come up again we are in* DORIS's *room. She is on the bed, just coming to. He is on the chair next to her.*)

(*Still half-unconscious.*) Rossano, Rossano, kiss me. Kiss me, Rossano, when in Paris kiss me. Kiss me.

> (*He leans down to kiss her. She comes to.*)

Oh. Oh!! (*She slaps him hard.*)

ROSSANO. But, but Doris, my darling.

DORIS (*jumping up*). I am not your darling. I am a

citizen of the United States of America, the greatest little country in the world. And I demand to know what is going on around here!

ROSSANO. But don't you remember? The balcony? (*He whistles a quick bar of "their" balcony song.*)

DORIS. Oh dear. Oh my gosh. Oh golly. Oh, of course. Oh Rossano, I apologize. Oh what a scene it must have been. I'm so sorry, Rossano. (*She giggles.*)

ROSSANO. How do you feel?

DORIS. Feel? I feel fine. Rossano, shouldn't I feel fine? Nothing happened, did it? We didn't *do* anything? I didn't *say* anything, did I?

ROSSANO. Of course not.

DORIS. Of course not. How could I even think such a thing? I'm such a ninny, Rossano.

ROSSANO. May I say something to you very personal?

DORIS. Not *too* personal, I hope.

ROSSANO. Something I am feeling?

DORIS. Yes?

ROSSANO. Your eyes?

DORIS. My eyes?

ROSSANO. My mother was blue. Blue like you.

DORIS. Oh. I don't know what to say.

ROSSANO. Say nothing. Say nothing, my darling.

(*He leans over to kiss her. She allows a small kiss.*)

DORIS. Oh, Rossano, there's something I'd like to show you.

ROSSANO. What is that?

DORIS. Would you walk to the other side of the room?

ROSSANO. The other side of the room? Away from you? But why? Is it an American custom?

DORIS (*coyly*). You'll see.

ROSSANO. Well, if you insist. What else should I do? Hold my hands over my head?

DORIS. You can hold your nose if you want to. Some people prefer.

(*He does. She turns her ass to him and the audience, tilts it coyly, and farts a long thin fart. Then she looks to him to see how he liked it.*)

Well, what do you think?

ROSSANO. Very, very nice.

DORIS. I'm glad you liked it.

ROSSANO. I want another kiss.

DORIS. Oh, Rossano, you musn't.

(*He kisses her again. After the kiss she keeps her eyes closed and he takes out a long, sharp knife.*)

ROSSANO. Doris. Doris, my darling, open your eyes and look at what I have.

DORIS. Oh, Rossano. It's . . . it's so big. Very big. Very big and sharp. What is it?

ROSSANO. It's a knife. Very big and sharp. One of the best in Paris.

DORIS. What do you Parisians do with that?

ROSSANO. It is for giving pleasure to young American ladies.

DORIS. Oh, but Rossano, I couldn't.

ROSSANO. Why not. Let yourself go. You are in Paris and it is young and we are spring.

DORIS. No. I don't do that. (*This last is a bit hysterical.*)

ROSSANO. Just a little bitty nick. Just a little nicky-nick.

DORIS. Will you put it away after that?

ROSSANO. Don't you trust me?

DORIS. Of course I trust you, Rossano. I'm a very trusting girl.

ROSSANO. Well, then.

(*He nicks a bit of her arm. She feels no pain but reacts to the marring and resulting imperfection of her self.*)

DORIS. Rossano, look, I'm bleeding.

ROSSANO. Yes, I see. You have the most beautiful blood.

DORIS. That's very nice but I'm afraid this will have to stop. I think we've had enough, just about enough.

ROSSANO. It is only the beginning.

DORIS. My father is a minister.

ROSSANO (*stabbing her again*). All Paris shines for you tonight.

DORIS. Rossano! Stop it. They won't take me back this way. They won't recognize me. They won't believe it.

(*He stabs her again, always smiling, always cool.*)

I think I'm afraid.

ROSSANO.   When in Paris—(*He stabs.*)

DORIS.   My name is Doris. I am pert. I am pretty. I am an American. I don't know anything about this.

ROSSANO.   I will teach you. (*He stabs.*)

DORIS.   Doris. Doris, it's going to be O.K. You're going to wash this right out of your hair. (*She puts her hand to her hair, finds blood.*) My hair! My hair is blonde. I am an airline stewardess in a plane that *never* crashes but only almost. This is only almost. The American Legion is going to come on horses with trumpets and the President is going to give me a medal at the end and I'm going to be happy again just singing in the rain, just singing—what a marvelous feeling—what a strange mood I'm in—

(*He stabs her several times.*)

I'm America's Honeybunch!

ROSSANO (*leaving*).   Au revoir, Miss Prettyasabutton. This time, c'est la vie.

DORIS (*on the floor, in increasing fear*).   But the other man, the nice one, is coming to save me. I'm always saved. Someone will come. I'll be all right. Everything's coming up roses, Doris. Doris. Doris, take hold of yourself. I'm going to wash that man right out of my hair. I'm going to—I'm alone. Doris. Some enchanted evening you will see? meet? see? a stranger. But I'm Doris. I love Paris in the springtime when it drizzles. Doris. I'm alone. Help me. Forgive me. I'm alone. I can't die. Doris can't die. Die? Die? I'm dying. *I* am dying. Really dying. I'm really——.

(*She screams loudly in fear.*

Curtain.)

THE GOLDEN SCREW
or
That's Your Thing, Baby
Tom Sankey

Playbill for Premiere Production

THE GOLDEN SCREW

or

That's Your Thing, Baby

written and composed by Tom Sankey

Presented at Theatre Genesis
(St. Mark's Church-in-the-Bouwerie, New York City)

Directed by Robert Siegler

CAST

GRANDMA ....Janet Day

CAP AND TINKER ....Murray Paskin, Patrick Sullivan

ARMY-NAVY STORE ....Murray Paskin

JOHN BURKE ....Patrick Sullivan

MILLIE ....Janet Day

UNEMPLOYMENT OFFICE ....Murray Paskin

BEN AND BETTY ....Janet Day, Murray Paskin

NEWPORT FOLK FESTIVAL....Janet Day, Murray Paskin,
Patrick Sullivan

SUSY BARTHOLOMEW ....Janet Day

SIMON SEZ ....Murray Paskin

COCKTAIL PARTY ....Janet Day, Murray Paskin,
Patrick Sullivan

POET ....Patrick Sullivan

FIRST MUSICIAN ....Tom Sankey

SECOND MUSICIAN ....Jack Hopper

THE INNER SANCTUM..........Kevin and Jerry Michael,
Frank Thumhart, Vince Taggart

(Editor's note: Some of the parts listed above were eliminated in editing the version of *The Golden Screw* printed in this volume.)

Scenic designer: Charles Lewis
Lighting designer: Kit Jones
Technical director: Kit Jones
Stage manager: Mollie Snyder
Lighting manager: Timothy Oksman

TOM SANKEY

"The biography of *The Golden Screw:*

"Originally done as a workshop production in short form for Theatre Genesis in June 1966. Was accepted for production (in Genesis' regular program) and rewritten and expanded during July. Opened as regular Theatre Genesis off-off-Broadway production September 16 (the first production under a Federal research grant given to St. Marks).

"Murray Paskin, Janet Day, Jack Hopper and I all performed in the original workshop production. Patrick Sullivan and the Inner Sanctum joined the full length production as done at the church.

"Original scheduled run of 3 weekends, 9 performances, was extended an additional weekend for 5 more performances. Usual audience for the usual run is a total of 600. We played to an estimated 1,500 and turned away an additional 2,000.

"Picked up first off-Broadway producer at last performance and lost her during the following week.

"Accidentally met agent (Carolyn Jenks), an old friend from college and early days in NYC at performance of another play the following weekend. Jenks arranged for 2 producer's auditions. Picked up second producer and Channel 13 interest.

"Taped show for Channel 13 on October 18, and lost second producer same night.

"Howard Smith of *Village Voice* saw taping, called Jerry Wexler of Atlantic Records. Auditioned for Atlantic and David Eliscu and Paul Stoudt (the eventual off-Broadway producers) the same week that Channel 13 announced cancellation."*

* Editor's note: Although the expletive with which Sankey concluded his stage presentations was not used in the taped version, New York City's "Educational" Channel 13 cancelled a scheduled showing on the grounds that *The Golden Screw* was not "family" fare.

LIST OF SCENES AND SONGS

"Bad Girl"
1. Grandma
    "New Evaline"
2. Cap and Tinker
    "2000 Miles"
3. Army-Navy Store
    "Jesus, Come Down"
4. John Burke—Millie—Unemployment Office
    "You Won't Say No"
5. Ben and Betty
    "Beautiful People"
6. Newport Folk Festival
    "I Can't Make It Anymore"
    "Trip Tick Talking Blues"
7. Susy Bartholomew
    "Can I Touch You"
8. Simon Sez
    "That's Your Thing, Baby, It's Not Mine"
9. Cocktail Party
    "Here I Am on the Bottom End of Bleecker Street"
10. Poet
    "Little White Dog"

(*The stage is divided in two, stage left being at a
higher level than stage right. Stage right is used for
all the dramatic segments of the show and it holds
a table and several chairs, enough to seat the actors
between scenes and one or two extra for use as
props. Stage left is used by the musicians and it has
chairs and assorted folk instruments.*

*A minimum of actors is used, preferably three,
and they play all the parts in the dramatic segments,
dividing the parts between them in the most logical
way. During the play, the actors sit on chairs at
the rear of stage right, crossing down to center to
play their scenes and using small hand props and
chairs as required.*

*A minimum of four musicians is required. The
musical arrangements increase in complexity as the
play progresses, starting with simple folk accompaniment (guitar, autoharp, harmonica) and adding instruments from song to song (kazoo, tambourine,
second guitar, jug) until the second act when the
guitars and autoharp are electrified, backed up by
drums and electric bass. The first musician is the
lead singer and plays the autoharp. The second
musician is lead guitar, the third is percussion and
the fourth plays bass.*

*Before the play while the audience is being seated,
a recording of Jesse Fuller is heard. Before the music
runs out, the actors and musicians take their places
on stage. As the recorded music fades and the house
lights dim, a spotlight comes up on the first musician
and he begins the play by singing the first song.*)

SONG #1—"Bad Girl"

She's a bad girl, and her father works in the bank.
And her mother belongs to the Woman's Club
And her brother's in medical school.
She's a bad, bad girl.

She's a bad girl, and it's really a terrible shame.
She was in the honor society.
And was editor of the yearbook.
She's a bad, bad girl.

She's a bad girl, and I hope they never find out
That a girl who's the model of womanhood
Is heading for so much trouble.
She's a bad, bad girl.

She's a bad girl, and I wanted her for my own
But she said she would never love anyone
Who still wore pajamas to bed.
She's a bad, bad girl.

ACT I

SCENE 1

GRANDMA. Your grandfather started out as a musician, you know. I remember . . . back in Waukegan . . . it was before your mother or any of the kids were born . . . When your grandfather was playing in the pit orchestra at the . . . Orpheum Theatre.

I used to go down to the theatre when the show was over and meet him and we'd go out for a beer afterwards.

The first night . . . I walked down there . . . we'd just been married . . . and I went around to the stage door and the stage manager said I'd have to go around to the front and buy a ticket. And I said, "Oh, no, I'm Ole's

wife." And he said, "There's no Ole here." And I said,
"Yes, there is. He's the drummer in the orchestra and
I'm his wife." And he said, "Our drummer's name is Bill
Smith. You must have the wrong theatre."

Well, I didn't know what to do. So I thought maybe I
did have the wrong theatre. So I went over to the . . .
Rialto Theatre . . . I think . . . Yes. Well, I went over
there and, come to find out, he wasn't over there, either.
So I came back to the Orpheum, mad as a wet hen,
and I said, "He does too! I know he's working here at the
Orpheum." And he said, "Orpheum?"

I was so mad I could've spit green nickels. Just then
I hear a voice behind me saying, "What's the matter,
Jim? Do you want me to throw this floozy out for you?"

It was Ole. He'd put him up to the whole thing.

The son of a bitch.

SONG #2–"New Evaline"

On account of you the whole night long
Is spent in anxious speculation
On how I might arouse your sympathy . . .

> You sweet thing . . .
> You sweet thing . . .
> You sweet thing . . .
> You sweet thing, Evaline.

I'm flying tight around your head
With castinets and gifts of dust
And angry quiet urgings of my name.

> (*Chorus.*)

I awaken to a thousand cries
The agonies of pointless lust
The insubstantial presence of my dreams.

> (*Chorus.*)

A million times I've strangled you
I've shot you down, I've torn your face
But still you grow inside my freaking head.

> (*Chorus.*)

SCENE 2

TINKER. We can't do "Rye Whiskey" at the pep assembly. Mr. Stahlberg says we can't. It'll corrupt our fellow students, I guess.

CAP. Let's do "Cocaine Blues" instead.

(*They both laugh.*)

TINKER. We can't do that, either. The A Cappella Choir wants to do that.

CAP. Hey, they ought to let Miss Martinson sing that one. Wouldn't that be great? Old "Boobs" Martinson singing . . . (*Imitating operatic soprano.*) "Cocaine . . . run all 'round my brain."

TINKER. Ignore him. He runs down after a while. My problem, is, doctor . . . what are we gonna do instead? How about "Saints"? Well, Stahlberg likes that one. He says it's more fitting for a pep assembly.

CAP. It always makes a big hit.

TINKER. Everybody sings along . . .

CAP. They clap their hands.

TINKER (*to* CAP). Well, not everybody . . . just the teachers.

SONG #3—"2000 Miles"

The town I'm from is 2000 miles long. (*Repeat.*)
Since the day I left, everything I've done is wrong.
  (*Repeat.*)
Don't know how to cry, but I'll try to sing you this song.
  (*Repeat.*)

Came to the city just to see if I could change my luck.
Time goes by in a brainless trailer truck.
Tried to change the tune but I think my finger is stuck.

I'm getting up in the morning just to see the sun come in.
Go to bed at night just to air my moccasins.
I won a four star rating just from eating gelatin.

I'm going back to my lily-white, fastback Cadillac.

I'm gonna track that Cadillac back to its tar paper shack.
It's a three year trip but on Monday night I'll be back . . .

So don't sell my things 'cause on Monday night I'll be
    back . . .

You better wait for me, baby, 'cause on Monday night I'll
    be back . . .

SCENE 3

    (*The Army-Navy store salesman comes forward to
    greet a customer. He has a tape measure around
    his neck.*)
SALESMAN. Somebody taking care of you?
Sure. What size?
You sure? You look more like a thirty to me. Let's
just check it to make sure.
    (*He takes the tape, reaches it around an imaginary
    waist, looks, shrugs.*)
Well, you're right. Twenty-nine. Remember, they don't
shrink. Better make it a twenty-eight.
    (*He bends down, places one end of the tape on the
    floor, pushes the other end into an imaginary
    crotch, looks up disgusted.*)
Well, hold still, will ya? How can I get your length?
    (*He measures again, stands.*)
Let's see. Twenty-nine, thirty . . . better make it a
thirty. You like 'em a little long? Short? All right . . .
No, none of them shrink. Guaranteed. Nope. We don't
have anything that shrinks, unless you want olive drab
army pants.
Nope. If you want blue jeans, they don't shrink.
They're all sanforized, now days.
Well, if you want tight pants, buy tight pants. Here.
Let me just show you.
    (*He turns and goes upstage, returns immediately
    holding imaginary pants.*)
Here. These are guaranteed washable. Daks style.
These *are* right. Tight! I wear them myself. (*Indicates
his own pants.*)

Well, all right, then. If blue jeans is what you want, why don't you say so? Just a minute.

(*He crosses upstage again, comes down with more imaginary pants.*)

Here. How's this? We don't have the others in your size. No, these won't shrink, either. Won't fade, either. You want blue jeans that fade? Why don't you buy light blue jeans? Sure. We have pink blue jeans, too. We got green blue jeans.

All right. You'll take these?

(*He folds them, puts them on imaginary counter.*)

Now, what else can you use? Belts, ties? We got everything. We got a special on boxer shorts. Assorted patterns. Shirts? Sure. What size? Small? Medium? Medium. Okay, I have a beautiful button down . . .

(*He turns to go upstage; stops.*)

Hah? A work shirt you want? Do you work?

(*He's beginning to warm up and continues to gently tease the imaginary customer.*)

No. It's all right. I'll sell you anything you want. Blue work shirt. Okay. You want good quality, cheap, what?

I got one guaranteed to fade and shrink, but it costs a little more. How about that?

Oh, you don't want it to fade or shrink. Uh-huh. You want tight pants and loose shirts. Funny . . . years ago, it was the other way around. Okay, we got 'em. For a dollar nineteen. We got better ones for two dollars. How many? Okay, anything else?

Boots? Sure, we got all kinds of boots, galoshes. How about a nice pair of hip boots?

Yeah . . . *hip* boots. I got all kinds of hip boots. We got hip boots that come all the way up to your armpits. We don't want that kind, huh? What d'ya want?

Like the beatniks wear? Motorcycle boots. You seen 'em in the window? Okay. We have to go upstairs for that. Anything else you want from down here?

"An *engineer's* hat." What kind? You look like a . . . electronics engineer, right?

Railroad engineer? Yeah? You drive a train? No.

Listen, we have several railroad engineers who buy their hats here. They're good friends of mine. I wouldn't kid you. I know the kind of hats they wear . . .

(*He turns to go upstage.*)
We have a nice snap-brim straw hat with a green
feather for a dollar and a half.
(*He crosses upstage to his seat.*)

SONG #4—"Jesus, Come Down"

There once lived a man; a wild sort of man,
Who knew the terrors of the hunted.
They took him away and to this very day
They've nailed his body to the cross.

> Jesus!
> Jesus!
> Jesus, come down from that cross!

He chose to be, he wanted to be
The symbol of life everlasting.
But now we see, eternally,
The dead Christ nailed upon the cross.

(*Chorus.*)

Today men die and they don't know why
But the glory of death is something sacred.
But he knows why—I'm telling you why:
Because we worship death upon the cross.

(*Chorus.*)

Is this war like every other war?
Between the true believers and the heathen?
The peaceful way was thrown away
When he gave his body to the cross.

(*Chorus.*)

Everyone sees that war is a disease
And yet we march off to death with flags a-waving.
But we cannot cure it; we must endure it
While he's still hanging on the cross.

(*Chorus.*)

SCENE 4

(*New York City Unemployment Office* SUPERVISOR
crosses down to center, holding some forms.)

SUPERVISOR. Are you the person who refuses to stand
in Line O? Well?

No, I'm sorry. The rules state that if you do not report
in on your assigned day, you must stand on Line O.

No, you may not mail in the form unless you take a
job and are working on the day you normally report.

Where does it say that?

(*Looking through papers.*)

Oh, I see. It says here that on last Tuesday you re-
ported for work as a hog slopper at Mergendieler's Pig
Farm in Utica, New York.

Well, that's all very well, but it states on your original
application that you are a . . . pearl diver?

Well, what is it? If the position you are officially un-
employed from is "dishwasher" you must enter that in
the appropriate space on your original application. I must
warn you that the penalties for wilfully misrepresenting
the facts are very stiff. At any rate, you must apply for
the position of dishwasher or pearl diver as the case may
be.

You say you applied for the position of caster of pearls
before swine but all you could get was hog slopper?
Very funny. Stand on Line O.

(*He returns to his seat.*)

SONG #5—"You Won't Say No"

When the rhythm of the room brings us toegther,
    Oh . . . no, you won't say no.
When your eyes brush mine, the moment lasts forever.
    Oh . . . no, you won't say no.
And the cigarette I light for you ignites a private spell
With our hands still touching as the match burns out.
Then that touch betrays the hopes of newfound lovers.
    Oh . . . no, you won't say no.

Through the ritual of now I go parading.
Oh . . . no, you won't say no.
With the sounds of nonsense speech already fading.
Oh . . . no, you won't say no.
For my fantasies project me to a night of scorching touch
With a certain magic promise of success.
When the party breaks, I know I'll find you waiting.
Oh . . . no, you won't say no.

SCENE 5

(BEN *and* BETTY *move to center; he sits and she
stands next to him.* BEN *is a portly, middle aged
Broadway promoter. He is coarse, stupid and extremely nervous.* BETTY *is plump and bosomy with
bleached hair and purple eyelids. She flutters and
gushes a lot.*)

BEN (*trying to be very charming*). Come on in,
kiddo, sit down. Ya want a coffee? Hey, Betty, you wanna
tell him or should I?

BETTY. Let me tell ya, my husband is the world's
worst secret keeper. If he's got a surprise for somebody,
he's gotta walk around all day with his fly open.

BEN (*embarrassed and flattered*). Aw-w-w-w-w-w-w
. . .

BETTY. No kidding. Everytime he's got a big deal to
spring on someone, he walks in with his fly wide open.

BEN. Hey, ya want a cup of coffee?

BETTY. He's still a lover, though. Fourteen years
we've been married and he's still a lover. Go ahead and
tell him, Ben.

BEN. Now, will ya . . . do you have to give the whole
thing away, Betty?

BETTY. Listen. We listened to your tape . . .

BEN. I'm the one can't keep a secret!

BETTY. Some of your songs are just beautiful!

BEN. Go ahead, spill the beans.

BETTY. No kidding!

BEN. Hey, Betty! You're walking around with your
fly wide open!

BETTY. Oh, that's a good one, Benny. Listen, the day

I walk around with my fly open is the day I leave you. No, really—Ben is the only one who's ever worn the pants in our family.

BEN. Aw-w-w-w-w-w-w-w-w . . .

BETTY. He wears the pants, but he gives me the hot pants!

BEN (*calling*). Hugo—that coffee here yet?

BETTY. Fourteen years and he's still a lover.

BEN. You getting a little hungry.

BETTY. To tell you the truth, we're a little nervous about one or two of those songs, though.

BEN. Oh, brother!

BETTY. Especially the one about . . .

BEN. Especially the one about screwing.

BETTY. The one where you say "I'm gonna screw you . . ." . . . they might not play it on the radio.

BEN. Maybe you could change the words a little.

BETTY. Don't get me wrong, I *love* the song.

BEN. We love the whole thing. Ter-riffic!

BETTY. We've been playing the tape for everybody. Our kids love it.

BEN. All except the one about screwing. I didn't play that one for them.

BETTY. With a voice like yours and with these songs . . .

BEN. All except that one about screwing.

BETTY. Ben's afraid it'll give me hot pants.

BEN. Aw-w-w-w-w-w-w-w . . .

BETTY. Fourteen years and he's still jealous!

BEN. Isn't she terrific!

SONG #6—"Beautiful People"

1. When I was young I had a vision
      Of the beautiful people—the beautiful people.
   I knew that I would find them someday:
      The beautiful people—the beautiful people.
   Somewhere there were people with hope in their eyes
   And sweet love in their hearts for everybody.
   I prayed to God that they would take me,
      Those beautiful people.

2. At last I found where they were hiding,
     The beautiful people—the beautiful people.
   They lie beneath a giant shadow,
     The beautiful people—the beautiful people.
   They cringe beneath a cruelty that blots out the sun
   And the hope in their eyes is quickly dying.
   Is there no way that we might save them?
     Those beautiful people.

3. Now they are gone and no one mourns them,
     The beautiful people—the beautiful people.
   Their love and hope have perished with them,
     The beautiful people—the beautiful people.
   For the beautiful people are within us, my friends,
   And our own fear is the killer we have welcomed.
   The wasted dream: that we might all be
     Those beautiful people.

SCENE 6

(Three folksingers, DAVE, EARL, JEANIE, *cross to
center, bringing two chairs with them. They arrange the chairs around an imaginary table, leaving a space D.C. for a fourth person.*

*They are in a bar in Newport, the afternoon
before one of the evening concerts of the annual
folk festival.*

*As the scene starts, they try to attract the
attention of someone who has just entered. The
bar is crowded and they shout to be heard.)*

DAVE *(standing and waving).* Hey! There he is!

EARL *(waving).* GET HIM OVER THERE.

DAVE. Hey! Top Forty!

EARL. Come on over, little buddy.

JEANIE *(to* DAVE). Why don't you wave your twelve
string guitar at him?

DAVE *(to* JEANIE). Why don't you wave your beautiful long black hair at him. Or, why don't you wave one
of your big, beautiful . . .

EARL *(cutting him off).* He sees us. Come on over
here! You owe us a beer.

DAVE (*gesturing to a waitress*). Miss! Four more beers right here!

JEANIE. Hello, darling! I just knew you wouldn't forget.

DAVE. He wouldn't forget. He's here to stampede the herd.

JEANIE. Everyone's been having a tremendous fight over the "Beautiful People" song.

DAVE. Aren't you sorry you wrote it? I mean, it must be a terrible drag, all that money, and being so popular and all . . .

EARL. And everybody jumpin' on the bandwagon . . .

SONG #7—"I Can't Make It Anymore"

Doo-doo doo-doo doo-doo doo-doo doo-doo doo-doo doo.
I can't make it anymore, pal, I can't make it anymore.

Me and Frank were down on Fourth Street.
Hittin' the cars when they stopped for the light.

I had a pint of muscatel.
Frank was pretty far gone already.

Frank had just got out of Bellevue.
All wrapped up with adhesive tape.

His face was grey his eyes were bloodshot.
Scarin' the tourists going home from the Village.

All of a sudden he sat on the curb.
Shivering, shuddering there on the curb.

I said, "Come on, Frank, just a little longer."
He said, "I can't make it anymore, pal."

I said, "Come on, Frank, I'll take ya to the Mission.
They'll call a doctor, they'll see you're sick."

Frank fell over, his head in the gutter.
His feet was kickin, his mouth was droolin.

I walked away and left him lyin.
I left him there, I knew he was dyin.

Doesn't anybody care about me?
I had a pal, but he has left me.

Why'd ya leave me, Frank?
I need ya, Frank.
I can't make it without you.
I can't make it anymore.

I can't make it anymore, pal, I can't make it anymore.

Doo-doo doo-doo doo-doo doo-doo doo-doo doo-doo doo.

> (*At the conclusion of the song, the house lights
> come up, the performers relax and come off the
> stage for intermission.*
> *During the intermission, amplifiers, speakers and
> microphones are set up on stage left for electrical
> guitar, bass, autoharp, harmonica, etc. Additional
> percussion instruments are set in place.*
> *After the intermission, the audience is seated and
> the performers return to the stage. The musicians
> take their places and begin tuning up. At first the
> sound is random and noisy, then begins to solidify
> into a steady beat until they are into the first
> number. The house lights dim, lights come up on
> stage left, and song #8 begins.*)

SONG #8—"Trip Tick Talking Blues"

1. When the treasury department sends a form
   That says you paid no taxes the year you were born
   And that they figure the money due
   Along with all the interest accrued
      Amounts to one million, four hundred and ninety-
      three thousand, two hundred and twenty-nine dollars
      and fifteen cents, including tip.
   Why don't you . . .
   Take a little trip?
      (Why don't you get yourself straightened out?)

2. When an accident near the recruiting station
   Results in your left leg's amputation
   And you cannot return to college in the fall,

So you lose your deferment and get your draft call . . .
   And they won't let you be a conscientious objector
   because you're a Sunday school dropout,
Why don't you . . .
Take a little trip?
   (On your crutches . . . maybe in your wheelchair . . .)

3. Now, if you happen to go out after dark
   And you don't get mugged while out in the park,
   Watch out! The cops'll figure you
   To be one of the muggers and they'll mug you.
     Furthermore, if you're afraid of being arrested for
     either spitting or *not* spitting in the subway . . .
     they've got laws against both . . .
   Why don't you . . .
   Take a little trip?
     (You can get above all that, you know . . . and you
     don't have to walk, either . . .)

4. While being knocked down by a crosstown bus
   I had a momentary loss of consciousness
   Due to the bus backing up again
   And exhausting all over me, so then
   I had a dream-like meditation
   While receiving mouth-to-mouth resuscitation
   From a Meter Maid. I dreamt
   I caught a fatal dose of trenchmouth, which sent
     Me up to the Pearly Gates. Well, St. Peter came
     out and looked me over. Then he shook his hoary
     head and said:
   "Why don't *you* . . .
   Take a little trip?"
     (Well, I said, "No thanks. That sounds like a bad
     trip.")
     (Bye-bye . . . don't forget to write . . . that's all.)

ACT II

SCENE 7

(SUSY BARTHOLOMEW, *a young pretty Village girl, crosses down to the chair and sits with her feet up as though she were sitting up in bed.*)

SUSY. Oh! (*She smiles.*) I was waiting for you and I fell asleep. What time is it?

No wonder.

(*She lights a cigarette.*)

How did it go? No, wait a minute. Give me a minute to wake up. Did you take a cab home? Of course. You always take a cab. Did you eat?

That's good.

What? What else did you have. You mean, right in the studio? It must have been quite some little banquet. Did you bring me anything? Oh.

(*Pretends to go back to sleep.*)

All right.

(*She makes an obvious effort to brighten up.*)

I'm awake now. Now, what? Oh, yes. How did it go?

Is that all you're going to say? Is that what I woke up for?

Do you have to do any of the songs over again?

I shouldn't think so. You've been there since yesterday noon. Remember the first time when you had to record everything in four hours?

Don't say that. That's still my favorite record.

Well, something must have gone wrong. You're depressed again.

Yes you are. *I* can tell when you're depressed. So what is it?

You're happy with all the songs, aren't you? The play-back was good, wasn't it?

Let's see, then. You're depressed because the President isn't following your advice. The cab driver didn't recognize you? No? Well, if that's not it, it must really be something big. I know. You're bored. All the suspense is gone. You're a big star . . . everything comes easy . . . every record is a hit . . .

Oh, you've tasted success and it's like drinking champagne from a lady's slipper and then you find she uses Mexana Foot Powder. It's time for a change.

Change your socks . . . change your underwear . . . Change your hat! Wear a propeller beanie.

Why don't you get a new suit? Maybe one of those Carnaby Street jobs with epaulettes and shoulder braid . . . and some bright red boots with high heels and open toes.

Oh, that appeals to you, does it?

You could take up a new instrument. A sousaphone. No, a tuba! A singing tuba player!

Maybe you could take those numerous suggestions about singing lessons. You could sing like Robert Goulet. You'd have all those fat, middle-aged ladies in love with you.

Oh, it's going to be wonderful and exciting. But I think you're also pretty tired, so maybe you'd better come to bed.

Come on. Take off those old things and throw them away. In the morning, we'll turn you into a new person. We'll change you all around . . .

But that's for the morning. I want the same old you in bed with me tonight.

I hope I like the new you.

(*She goes to sleep. The lights fade.*
She returns to her place upstage.)

SONG #9—"Can I Touch You"

The cigarettes we shared
   have left a poison in the air
   that seems to penetrate each thing I say
   and burn all thoughts of love away.
How can I hope to reach you there
   while we are chained to a despair

that all's been given
and nothing taken.

Can I touch you, honey, can I touch you?

How I have yearned to see the time
    when all the flowers of your mind
    would just be offered as a gift of love
    and not taken as a prize of love.
But there's a phony kind of light
    that makes you think you've got the right
    to turn it on or off.
    How long can you keep faking?

Can I touch you, honey, can I touch you?

It's enough to drive a man insane,
    I've brought you all my private pains
    and watched you wash and hang them out to dry,
    returned them for a fresh supply.
You seem to think I have a scheme
    to take away your precious dream
    and I just want to share
    the plans that you are making.

Can I touch you, honey, can I touch you?

Wontcha come on down for just a while
    and listen to the words that I'll
    be saying to that private lover's face
    another time another place?
It's such a drag to be a fraction
    of a second off the track
    discovering it's only
    half a heart you're breaking.

Can I touch you, honey, can I touch you?

SCENE 8

——————

(SIMON SEZ, *the disc jockey, crosses to the chair and
sits. He wears dark glasses and a straw hat. When*

on the air, SIMON *is hysterically happy and addresses himself to his control room D.R. When speaking to his visitors, his normal voice is rough and glum.)*

SIMON SEZ *(holding microphone; to control room).* Hey-hey! Today's the day! This is the place: right here and right there! You're plugged in to the hits! You're plugged in to the big sound! You're plugged in to "Simon Sez" and Simon says: "It's a hit!"

(He points to the control room as a signal for the engineer to start a record. We hear the first few beats of a rock and roll song, then he gestures to cut the sound in the studio and turns center and speaks in his normal voice to his visitor.)

Okay, glad you could make it. It's all right, the mike's dead, now. I'll let you know when to shut up. Sit down and let's talk. First of all . . .

(He raises his glasses for sincerity, flashes a phony smile.)

Pleased to meetcha, pal!

(He drops the glasses and flashes the smile.)

Next, let's get down to business. I've been a lot of help to you. I gave you your first play on the air, right? I've pushed every one of your singles, right? I've given you my "Hot Hit" designation three times now, right? Oh, I admit it was completely unsolicited, but it's put a lot of shekels in your pocket, and let me say . . .

(He raises his glasses and smiles.)

Nobody deserves it more than you, pal!

(Drops the glasses and the smile.)

Now I want my pound of flesh.

I've been scratchin' your back for a long time, now it's your turn to scratch mine.

(He turns to control room.)

Jerry, go right into the R.C. commercial, then use the first taped promo and I'll do the "Sound Bomb" live on "The Bees."

(Turns back to center.)

I like to choose winners. I like to choose winners and I like the winners to choose me.

I'm not asking much. I want to be the M.C. for your next Forest Hills concert.

I'm not a promoter of folk singers, I'm a promoter of pop singers. If you think you're getting rich off of the folkniks, you're sadly mistaken. The only folkniks at that concert will be standee—if there's room for them—after I fill the place with kids. You think about it.

Think about it this way: there's millions of kids calling you person to person and I'm the operator. Are you going to accept the call?

(*He looks to the control room, sees a signal, signals back. Over the speaker comes the whistle of a falling bomb.* SIMON *grabs the mike and shouts.*)

The latest from "The Bees"! "Love with a Capital H!" Simon says it's a *Sound Bomb!*

(*Sound of a bomb exploding blending into the opening beat of a record. It's cut off abruptly as* SIMON *turns back to center.*)

Deal? Done. Now, don't treat me like a hired man while we're up there. We're gonna be buddies, right? We're gonna be bosom buddies. Tell you what I'll even do for you. I'll trade in my trademark—my hat—for one of yours. Everybody knows what a big thing my hat is to me, so I'm laying my life on the line for you. That oughta go over pretty well. I've got it—you can present me with a new hat on stage—and I'll accept it. Bring along one of those crazy hats, okay?

SONG #10—"That's Your Thing, Baby, It's Not Mine"

> The fat lady on the crosstown bus
> Tries to make it at the evening rush.
> She's under the back seat having fun
> Collecting all the old chewing gum.
>   Well, that's your thing, baby, it's not mine.
>
> In the tattooing parlor, the tattooed man
> Is designing every kind of snake he can.
> His greatest achievement, when he was young,
> Was to tattoo a cobra on his tongue.
>   Well, that's your thing, baby, it's not mine.
>
> In the Emerald City, the Wizard sings:
> "I'd escape all this, if I had wings.

Come around, little girl . . . in the afternoon
And I'll give you a ride on my big balloon."
  Well, that's your thing, baby, it's not mine.

The Cardinal continues in his search
For additional funds to build his church.
The cathedral spire is a testament
To the passions buried in the cement.
  Well, that's your thing, baby, it's not mine.

The window dresser at the wiener works
Is writing the menu while the coffee perks.
He'd like to devour everything he's got.
His mind is full, but his stomach is not.
  Well, that's your thing, baby, it's not mine.

The needle dealer has a desperate plan
To end his love affair with the man.
He'll shoot up with nitro just before the raid
And blow up everybody when the dues are paid.
  Well, that's your thing, baby, it's not mine.

Casey Jones has himself a time
Riding the throttle on ninety-nine
His fantasy is (if he can only cut loose)
To catch up to and ram his own caboose.
  Well, that's your thing, baby, it's not mine.

I found my thing on 42nd Street
In the men's room where all the perverts meet.
I unzipped my zipper only to find
I had it with me all the time.
  Where's your thing, baby, I found mine.

SCENE 9

(CAROL, TIGER and RICHARD *cross D.C. They're at a
cocktail party talking to a fourth guest.* CAROL *is a
frivolous pop society model:* TIGER *is dumb—a rock
and roll dancer, he never stops moving:* RICHARD *is
an effeminate intellectual. They are all trying to be
hip insiders of the pop-camp scene.)*

RICHARD. I'm interested in some of the influences on you as an artist. The Rolling Stones—that's obvious.

CAROL. And the Beatles!

RICHARD. Uh . . . not quite so obvious. What I'm talking about is more like the influence of, say, Buddy Holly.

TIGER. Hey, he's great.

RICHARD. Ah . . . for his time, yes.

CAROL. John Lee Hooker, don't you think?

RICHARD. Oh, Carol, come *on*. You might as well say Sonny Terry—you always do.

TIGER. That one number you do. That "Shake 'Em Up" one? Reminds me of something the Ink Spots used to do.

CAROL *and* RICHARD. The Ink Spots!

TIGER. Well, I mean, like . . . sort of . . .

RICHARD. I knew it, Tiger, you're tone deaf. All you hear is the noise.

TIGER. All I hear is the beat.

RICHARD. Well, anyway . . .

TIGER. All I care is if I can dance to it. (*Referring to another part of the room.*) Hey! They're turning on in there!

RICHARD. Where? Are they?

CAROL. Oh, let's do it! I love pot! It turns me *on*.

TIGER. Hey, that's good, too, Carol!

RICHARD (*as they turn to go*). Do you indulge? This is the high point of the party, you know. (*He giggles.*)

(*They eagerly rush away and return to their seats.*)

SONG #11—"Here I Am on the Bottom End of
Bleecker Street"

1. I started off by playing the fool
at the outer edge of the wading pool,
now here I am on the bottom end of Bleecker Street.

2. The midnite riders fail to state
the reason for their after date
and here I am on the bottom end of Bleecker Street.

3. The Minetta Stream, so I've been told,
runs beneath the street of gold
but here I am on the bottom end of Bleecker Street.

4. The Perry Winkles are flashing by
   and wheeling around for a second try
   and here I am on the bottom end of Bleecker Street.

5. I ran into my sister Sal,
   I said, "It's time to be a pal,
   Here I am on the bottom end of Bleecker Street."

6. The subway saviour does a dance
   and dies without a second chance
   and here I am on the bottom end of Bleecker Street.

7. The dumb waiter is going around
   putting the civil service down
   and here I am on the bottom end of Bleecker Street.

8. There's a two-four-two on the narrow gauge
   bearing down with a mighty rage
   and here I am on the bottom end of Bleecker Street.

9. The neon grocery tried at last
   to penetrate the foggy past
   but here I am on the bottom end of Bleecker Street.

10. The saw horses sleep on their feet
    while barricading the jungle beat
    and here I am on the bottom end of Bleecker Street.

11. I don't know when I turned the bend
    but a subway sign is a girl's best friend
    and here I am on the bottom end of Bleecker Street.

12. The sewer cleaner turned away
    "The master isn't in today"
    here I am on the bottom end of Bleecker Street.

13. The chimney sweep waved as I passed.
    He said, "This time will be the last."
    Here I am on the bottom end of Bleecker Street.

14. The body snatcher laughed at me.
    "I knew you when," he said to me.
    Here I am on the bottom end of Bleecker Street.

15. There's a dying horse in the parking lot
    and nobody ever heard the shot
    and here I am on the bottom end of Bleecker Street.

SCENE 10

(The POET *crosses down and stands staring at a visitor. He rubs his face, shakes his head, continues to stare. He walks over to one side, staring, comes back to center.)*

POET. What am I supposed to do, wet my pants?
I did already.

Once upon a time I had a hundred dollar bill. I forget how I got all that bread—I just remember that I went down to the bank and bought myself a hundred dollar bill just to see what it was like.

I took my hundred dollar bill home and put it on the kitchen table and I sat and looked at it for a long time. Then I rolled it up into a little ball and I carefully inserted it into my rectum and I went out.

I walked around all day with that hundred dollar bill up my ass and I felt like king shit. I would say to people: "Hey, I have a hundred dollar bill up my ass."

(Disdainfully snaps his fingers.)

Then I began to worry. I began to imagine that it might get stuck in there. I might go for days, not being able to get it out, not being able to crap, I'd start to swell up and these horrible pains would be in my gut and I'd get all blue in the face, gasping for breath, and I'd have to go to Bellevue and be operated on.

And what then? Some sneaky doctor would steal my hundred dollar bill. Or maybe they'd just keep it to pay for the removal. And all those queer interns and nurses pointing at me and giggling. My picture in the Daily News!

I couldn't go to the hospital. I'd die first.

(Picturing headlines.)

"Strange Case of Fatal Monetary Suffocation. First Known Incident in New York City."

Nothing like that happened, of course. I removed it by natural means. I gave it to my landlord for two months rent without bothering to clean it off.

But it cured me. Completely. Never again did I stuff

money up my ass. And that's more than a lot of people can say.

(*Staring at his visitors again.*)

You're a sick cat, you know that? You've got everything you ever wanted and now you don't want it. That's *sick*, baby!

Now . . . let's see about the cure. Let me prescribe a little pill.

Gee whizzy-poo, Granny . . . pick the fucking wax out of your ears. Listen to the sound of change. I don't mean the electric tinny boom R and Arse music sound, although that's part of it . . .

I mean the pulsing, throbbing, rumbling sound of change, sir!

There *is* a revolution going on. And I don't mean the civil rights thing or the peace thing or the turning on routine or serving drinks to homosexuals bit, but something bigger, something underneath, something pushing all these other things ahead of it.

What am I talking about! I'm talking about you and me. I'm talking about the big business! The big *all*. The big *one*. Mankind, at long last, is developing *soul*!

Pick up on that! Tune in, friend. Your cells can feel it. You're changing, too. You got it inside you. Grab it! Grab it!

Your music tells me you know it, even though the words are fuzzy, the feeling is behind them, pushing.

It's more than revolution, it's evolution! It's happening *now*. The freaks of the world are seen to be normal and the madness that has held the world is dissolving. The cosmic consciousness is groping its way into every brain pan and some will embrace it with whoops of joy and some will lock it out with grunts of dry disgust, but the movement continues through ever-widening avenues of the great life! Now it's starting and before its tremendous cellular boom the ages of cold hard rusty rotten barriers will be tumbled and shredded and fed to the fires of the first life . . . the great total . . . the universal human soul!

(*During the last speech, a musical beat is heard, developing behind the* POET'S *words, one by one, all the musicians join in until a complete musical accompaniment is built up which continues after the speech and into the following musical number. The* POET *finishes with a great climax of voice and gesture and the light fades as the music swells.)*

SONG #12—Little White Dog"

Well, you think I'm flipping out . . .
But I'm really flipping in . . .
I've given you my blood . . .
Now, you're asking for my skin.

But I have a little message here
that was whispered in my mind
by my fairy godhead holy cow
for to tell to all mankind.

But I'm thinking most of you, my friends,
you're the first I'll tell it to:

I'm looking for . . . my little white dog . . .
I'm looking for . . . my little white dog . . .
I'm looking for . . . my little white dog . . .
Has anybody seen . . . my little white dog?

I'm looking for . . . that holy frail . . . (*Etc.*)

I'm looking for . . . my virgin eye . . . (*Etc.*)

I'm looking for . . . my little white dog . . . (*Etc.*)

(The spot fades on the first musician and the stage is dark. A spot rises on only the first musician's face (balance of stage and house blacked out). First musician stares blankly at audience, then lowers eyes, and speaks in a projected and baleful mutter: FUCK YOU. The lights come up again as the actors and musicians take their bows, the house lights come up and all the performers leave the stage.)

RED CROSS
Sam Shepard

Playbill for Premiere Production

RED CROSS

by Sam Shepard

Presented at Judson Poets' Theatre
(Judson Memorial Church, New York City)

Directed by Jacques Levy

CAST

CAROL ....Joyce Aaron

JIM ....Lee Kissman

MAID ....Florence Tarlow

Set design: Lindsey Decker
Set construction: Phil Harris
Lighting technicians: Stephen Lamb, Peter Nevraumont
Stage manager: Tony Holder
Assistant: Margret Hecht

SAM SHEPARD

"I was born inside a fort just outside Chicago and then raised in places all around the edge of Los Angeles but never right in it. I turned myself into an actor and came East in a red bus, acting all the way. I was dropped off in New York and teamed up with a painter kid that I knew before and had flown in while I was riding the bus all that time. I began experiments with various plants and growths that led to rhythm discoveries in space and time through packing up words and stretching them out along with their size and shape and sound. Once this got started lo and behold there came phantoms and ghosts speaking these words. At this point my acting stopped. I threw myself into an undefined region called OFF OFF BROADWAY which is a good enough name if you don't know where you're at. And things began to crackle. My credentials go like this: *Cowboys* and *Rock Garden* produced at Theatre Genesis. *Up to Thursday* produced at Theatre '67 (which changes its name every year) then later produced at the Cherry Lane Theatre. *4-H Club* produced at Theatre '65. *Dog* and *Rocking Chair* produced at Cafe La Mama. *Icarus' Mother* at the Caffe Cino and later at the Theatre Co. of Boston. *Red Cross* (which is what you're in for) at the Judson Church and directed by the notorious Jacques Levy. *Fourteen Hundred Thousand* at the Firehouse Theatre of Minnesota and later on NET TV (Channel 13 in New York and also coast to coast) so my mother got to see it. *Chicago* at again Theatre Genesis and later at the Martinique Theatre and meanwhile all over Europe, South America, Mexico, California and home again home again. *La Turista* at the American Place Theatre and soon to be released as a technicolor epic with Charlton Heston and Ruby Dee. Now settle back with a good cigarette a fresh Orange Crush and don't be afraid OF THE RED CROSS if it tends to drip on your lap. Bugaloo folks."

(*Scene: The bedroom of a cabin. There is a screen
door up center leading out to a small porch. A
window stage left and stage right. There are twin
beds, one under each window with the heads facing
upstage. The tops of trees can be seen through
the screen door and each of the windows to give
the effect of a second story. As the lights come up*
JIM *is sitting on the bed to stage left facing* CAROL
*who is sitting on the other bed. Everything in the
set plus costumes should be white.*)

CAROL. Look at it closely.

JIM. I am.

CAROL. You can't see it, then?

JIM. Yes.

CAROL. Then it *is* bad. I can't believe it. The tingling.
It's like a tingling thing under each eye. It goes into the
nose, too.

JIM. Maybe it's just sinus or something.

CAROL. No. I can see the results. If you can see something happening, then it couldn't be just sinus. The
whole face and ears and nose and eyes. And my hands.
Feel my hands.

(*She holds her hands out,* JIM *holds them.*)

JIM. Hm.

(*She pulls her hands back.*)

CAROL. Feel them? What's that, Jim. Something's
happening. My hands never sweat like that. And my feet.
Hold my foot.

(*She raises her foot,* JIM *holds it.*)

Just feel it. The other one, too. Feel them both. What's
that? Under the eyes is what bothers me. It's from wearing those glasses. I can tell. It's from the glasses. My
head aches so bad. I can't believe my head.

JIM. Why?

81

CAROL. It hurts. It's breaking open all the time. It crashes around inside.

(*She gets up and starts pacing around the stage as* JIM *remains sitting on the stage left bed.*)

JIM. What's the matter?

CAROL. It's anything. Beer or water or too many cigarettes and it starts to break. One day it'll break clear open and I'll die, I'll be dead then.

JIM. Take it easy.

CAROL. It might happen when I'm skiing or swimming.

JIM. There's always lots of people around those places. They'll see you and help.

CAROL. They'll see my head. (*She crosses to the stage right bed and stands on it facing* JIM *and begins to act out the rest as though she were skiing on a mountain slope.*) It'll be in the snow somewhere. Somewhere skiing on a big white hill. In the Rockies. I'll be at the top of this hill and everything will be all right. I'll be breathing deep. In and out. Big gusts of cold freezing air. My whole body will be warm and I won't even feel the cold at all. I'll be looking down and then I'll start to coast. Very slowly. I'm a good skier. I started when I was five. I'll be halfway down and then I'll put on some steam. A little steam at first and then all the way into the egg position. The Europeans use it for speed. I picked it up when I was ten. I'll start to accumulate more and more velocity. The snow will start to spray up around my ankles and across my face and hands. My fingers will get tighter around the grips and I'll start to feel a little pull in each of my calves. Right along the tendons and in front, too. Everything will be working at once. All my balance and strength and breath. The whole works in one bunch. There'll be pine trees going past me and other skiers going up the hill. They'll stop and watch me go past. I'll be going so fast everyone will stop and look. They'll wonder if I'll make it. I'll do some jumps and twist my body with the speed. They'll see my body twist, and my hair and my eyes will water from the wind hitting them. My cheeks will start to sting and get all red. I'll get further and further into the egg position with my arms tucked up. I'll look down and see the valley and the cars and houses and people walking up and down. I'll see all the cabins with smoke coming out the chimneys. Then it'll come. It'll start like a twitch in my left ear. Then I'll start to feel a throb in the bridge of my nose. Then a thump in the base of my neck. Then a crash right through my skull. Then I'll be down. Rolling! Yelling! All those people will see it. I'll be rolling with my skis locked and my knees buckled under me and my arms thrashing through the snow. The skis will cut into both my legs and I'll bleed all over. Big gushes of red all over the snow. My arms will be broken and dragging through the blood. I'll smell cocoa and toast and marmalade coming out of the cabins. I'll hear dogs barking and see people pointing at me. I'll see the road and college kids wearing sweat shirts and ski boots. Then my head will blow up. The top will come right off. My hair will blow down the hill full of guts and blood. Some bluejay will try to eat it probably. My nose will come off and my whole face will peel away. Then it will snap. My whole head will snap off and roll down the hill and become a huge snowball and roll into the city and kill a million people. My body will stop at the bottom of the hill with just a bloody stump for a neck and both arms broken and both legs. Then there'll be a long cold wind. A whistle, sort of. It'll start to snow a little bit. A very soft easy snow. The squirrels might come down to see what happened. It'll keep snowing very lightly like that for a long time until my whole body is covered over. All you'll see is this little red splotch of blood and a whole blanket of white snow.

VOICE OFFSTAGE. Miss Littles! Miss Littles, are you ready!

CAROL. What?

JIM. You have to go.

CAROL. Oh. Yes. (*She crosses to the door, she opens the door and yells down.*) I'll be right there! (*She crosses to* JIM *and kisses him on the forehead.*) You'll meet me, right? Please?

JIM. Yes.

CAROL. I'll see you then at six. (*She kisses him again.*) Six o'clock.

JIM. Right.

(*She exits.* JIM *gets up and crosses to the door, he hums some kind of tune, he looks out, then goes back to the bed and sits, he scratches his legs then he stands up and takes his pants off, he sits back down and starts scratching his legs, he starts picking little bugs out of his skin and then stepping on them, he gets up and starts doing pushups downstage center, a* MAID *appears on the porch through the screen door, holding two pillows, sheets, and bedspreads in her arms, she is rather fat and older than* JIM, *she watches* JIM *as he does his pushups, then she knocks on the door;* JIM *continues, she knocks again, then a third time very loudly.*)

(*Still doing pushups.*) Come in, come in, come in. Have a seat or something.

MAID.   It's the maid, dear.

JIM (*without turning to look*).   Come in, come in and have a bed or a seat. Whatever you want.

MAID (*still on the porch*).   I want to change the beds is all.

JIM (*he stops and turns to her, sitting on the floor*). Well, come in. The beds are in here.

MAID.   Thank you.

(*She enters and sets the linen down on the stage right bed,* JIM *sits on the floor looking at her.*)
I always seem to catch you, don't I?

JIM.   Yep. You catch me every time. I think you plan it.

MAID.   No.

JIM.   I think you do. You like catching me.

MAID.   It's just the time of day. You're the only one left this time of day.

JIM.   Come on. Where do they go?

MAID.   It's true.

JIM.   Where do they go? I've seen them around during the day. They hang around. They play tennis or something.

MAID.   I just make the beds.

JIM.   You know where they go. They go into town. Right?

(*She starts to change the stage left bed.*)
Hey, leave my bed alone! (*He stands.*)

MAID.   Well, I have to change it, dear.

JIM.   It's got stains. I don't want you to see the stains. I get embarrassed. (*He jumps on the stage left bed facing the* MAID.) I do. It embarrasses me. I get pink and everything.

MAID.   All right. (*She turns and starts making the other bed.*) I've seen yellow spots before, you know. It don't bother me.

JIM.   Well it bothers me. I get pink.

MAID.   I'm sorry about that.

JIM.   Do you know anything about crabs?

MAID.   About what?

JIM.   Crabs. Bugs that get in your pubic hair and eat your skin and suck your blood and make you itch.

MAID.   Like nits or something?

JIM.   What's a nit?

MAID.   Like lice.

JIM.   Yeah. Except on a smaller scale. Almost microscopic. With legs and red heads. They twitch when you grab hold of them. I can show you one if you want to see it. Do you want to see one?

MAID.   Not really.

JIM.   Oh, come on.

MAID.   All right.

(JIM *sits on the edge of the bed and picks at his legs, the* MAID *sits on the other bed facing him, he gets hold of a small bug and hands it carefully to the* MAID *who looks at it in the palm of her hand.*)

They must be part of the lice family to get in your skin.

JIM.   There. See it? They crawl around.

MAID.   Mm. You got these all over?

JIM.   No. They're localized.

MAID.   Can't you get some medicine? (*She hands the bug back to* JIM.)

JIM.   I don't want it back.

MAID.   Well, I don't want it.

JIM.   Throw it on the floor.

(*She throws it down,* JIM *steps on it.*)

What kind of medicine?

MAID.   Sheep dip or something.

JIM.   Sheep dip! (*He stands on the bed again.*) Why sheep dip!

MAID. I'm sorry. (*She starts changing the bed again.*)

JIM. Sheep dip is for woolly animals or dogs or something. Human lice are different from animal lice. The whole treatment is different.

MAID. Well that's the only thing I can tell you.

JIM. Who uses sheep dip for crabs? That's ridiculous. I mean that's really stupid.

MAID. Well I don't know, then. You'll have to find something pretty soon, though.

JIM. Why?

MAID. Well if I had parasites eating off me and draining me of all my blood and reducing my physical strength twenty-four hours a day, making me weaker and weaker while they got stronger and stronger, I can tell you that I'd do something. I'd get it taken care of. That's all I know. And I'm not smart.

JIM. You'd put sheep dip on them and kill your skin along with the crabs. Is that it?

MAID. I'd have enough sense to have my bed changed, knowing that crabs lay eggs inside the sheets and the blankets and that eggs hatch and that when eggs hatch new crabs are born. Baby crabs are born and baby crabs grow up like all crabs have to. And when they're grown they lay new crabs and it goes on and on like that indefinitely for years.

JIM. I'm talking about the immediate possibilities of killing the live crabs that are already there. Not the ones that haven't been born, maidy, maidy.

MAID. How 'bout a doctor?

JIM. Terrific. (*He jumps off the bed and crosses down center, doing arm exercises.*) I'm in the middle of the forest and you're talking about a doctor. Thank you. A country doctor, I suppose.

MAID. Isn't there someone to take you?

JIM. Not till six.

MAID. Can you wait?

JIM. I don't know. They really get to me every once in a while. You know what I mean? They pinch so hard I think they're going all the way through. They grab and squeeze. I think they must have teeth too. Along with the pinchers I think they have teeth.

MAID. Can you wait till six?

JIM (*he crosses right*). It's a long time to go on itching like this. To have any itchy skin, I mean. And they're moving up, too. They've gotten to my navel and yesterday I found one in my arm pit. Six is a long way off when this is happening to me. (*He crosses left.*) I can ignore them for periods of time. An hour at the longest if I'm preoccupied with something else. If I concentrate. They go away and then come back. It depends on the concentration. (*He stops doing the arm exercises.*)

MAID. I could take you. I have a car.

JIM. I climbed a tree yesterday and it went away for a couple of hours. I climbed all over the tree. Through the branches and clear up to the top. I sat up there for a couple hours smoking cigarettes. That did it for a while. Then I went swimming and that helped. Swimming always helps. Then I ran around the lake at a medium fast trot. I jogged all the way around. I got up a good sweat and I was breathing very hard and my heart was pounding. All the blood was going through me at once.

MAID. Have you had them for a long time?

JIM. I've had crabs for about ten years now and it gets worse every year. They breed very fast. It's nice, though. It's like having two bodies to feed.

MAID. Well I could take you. I have a car.

(JIM *turns to her.*)

Do you want to go now?

JIM. You drive in every day?

MAID. Well I don't walk.

JIM. You drive from town all the way into the middle of the forest to change somebody else's beds?

MAID. That's right.

JIM. Aren't there any beds in town?

MAID. I like the drive.

JIM. Me, too. It's nice. Calm. Smooth. Relaxing. Comfortable. Leisurely. Pleasurable. Enchanting. Delightful.

MAID. Yes.

JIM. Is there a doctor in town, did you say?

MAID. Well sure. I suppose. We could probably find one if you want to go.

JIM. There isn't one out here, huh? I mean they don't by any chance have a country doctor out in this neck of the woods. One a' them country guys in a Model T Ford and a beat-up leather bag full of sheep dip. Maybe even a veterinarian. I hear veterinarians can take as good care of you as a physician or a real doctor. Have you heard that?

MAID. Do you want to go into town or not?

JIM. Gee! I'd like the ride. I'd like that a lot. To ride in the car into town and get this taken care of. And then ride back. That'd be a lot of trips for you to take, though. A lot of extra hauls. Out and back and out and back. Coming and going.

MAID. I don't mind.

JIM. I could give you some gas money.

MAID. Forget it.

JIM. I insist. I absolutely insist.

MAID. Look—

JIM. Hey! Hold it! Hold it! I have an idea.

MAID. What?

JIM. You'll have to help me. Are you willing to help me?

MAID. I guess.

JIM. Okay. Come on. (*He starts pulling the stage right bed down center.*) Push. Push it.

   (*The* MAID *starts pushing the head of the bed as* JIM *pulls.*)

Come on, push. Push. Hup, hup.

MAID. What's this for?

JIM. You'll see. Come on. Get it down here. Hup, hup. Heave, ho!

MAID. I have to go pretty soon, you know.

JIM. It won't take long.

   (*They pull the bed downstage, then* JIM *crosses to the stage left bed.*)

Very good. Beautiful. Come on now. Help me with this. Come on. Hup, hup.

MAID. All right.

   (*They push the stage left bed across stage into the former position of the other bed.*)

What are you doing?

JIM. Rearranging. It'll be much nicer. Much, much nicer. More better for everyone concerned. Hup, two. Hup, two.

MAID. I don't know.

jim. Heave ho!
(*They get the bed into position, then* jim *crosses down to the other bed.*)
All right, maidy baby. The last lap. Come on. It's almost done. Have faith.
(*The* maid *crosses down to the bed and helps him push it stage left.*)
Heave, heave. Push, push. Put your back into it! A little more sweat there. Hup, two. At's it! Beautiful! Muy bien! Qué bonito!
(*He jumps on top of the stage left bed, the* maid *sits on the stage right bed facing him.*)
Esto es demasiado! (*He jumps up and down on the bed.*) Qué bello! Qué bello! Muy bien!

maid. Why did you do that?

jim (*he stops jumping*). Now I have a clean bed, right? A changed bed. Now, fresh, white, clean sheets imported from town. A downy, soft, airy pillow and a freshly washed bedspread. Guaranteed to be free of crabs and crab eggs and lice and ticks and nits. Guaranteed to smell sweet and pure. I have all this and you didn't even have to change my old bed. Isn't that nice? Now we don't have to go to town at all. We can stay here and jump around.

maid. Yes. (*She gets up and starts changing the stage right bed.*) And I'm all worn out.

jim. Now what are you doing! Leave that bed alone! Stop that!

maid. It's no longer yours, remember? We just switched. The one you're standing on is yours. You can't have both, you know. Make up your mind.

jim. It doesn't matter. Leave it alone! You'll catch something!

maid. You're getting very selfish, aren't you? You forgot somebody else sleeps in this bed. Somebody else who might not like to catch crabs.

jim. She doesn't care!
(*He flops down on the bed and lies on his stomach with his head toward the audience as the* maid *continues to change the stage right bed.*)

maid. I know she doesn't.

jim. Is this the last room you have?

MAID. Yep.

JIM. You save it for last?

MAID. No. I just make a point to come here last. I keep hoping one day I'll come and you won't be here. All I'll have to do is come into this room and make the beds and go right back out. One day I'll be able to do this room in no time at all and just go straight home. What a day that will be.

JIM. You go straight home from here?

MAID. That's right.

JIM. You don't hang around at all?

MAID. Nope.

JIM. You don't hang around to climb a tree or run around the lake or nothing? You should come at night, maidy. You'd like it better at night. We could go swimming.

MAID. No thanks.

JIM. It's really better at night. You'd be surprised the way it changes. All the different sounds and the air gets wetter. Sometimes it rains. That's the best time for swimming. When it rains. That way you get completely wet. A constant wetness.

MAID. Don't you catch cold?

JIM. No. Not a chance. Your body stays warm inside. It's just the outside that gets wet. It's really neat. I mean you can dive under the water and hold your breath. You stay under for about five minutes. You stay down there and there's nothing but water all around you. Nothing but marine life. You stay down as long as you can until your lungs start to ache. They feel like they're going to burst open. Then just at the point where you can't stand it any more you force yourself to the top. You explode out of the water, gasping for air, and all this rain hits you in the face. You ought to try it.

MAID. I'm too fat for swimming.

JIM. What do you mean? You won't sink. You just do the strokes, you know. (*He starts kicking his feet and stroking with his arms.*) You learn how to breathe and you kick and you stroke and there's nothing to it.

(*The* MAID *turns and looks at him.*)

You know how, don't you?

MAID. Not really. I can never put it all together. I mean I either stroke faster than I kick or visa versa.

JIM. Watch me. It's easy once you get started.

(*He starts going through the motions as the* MAID *watches.*)

The kicking is important. You have to keep your legs straight and kick from the waist. No bending the knees. And the arms too. Once the arm hits the water on the downsweep, you have to keep it straight. No bending from the elbow.

MAID (*she tries to copy him, moving her arms in an arc*). How do you keep your elbow straight?

JIM. Well no. Just as it goes through the water. That's the only time you have to worry. You can bend it as you take it back. Lie down over there and watch me.

(*She lies down on the stage right bed with her head toward the audience, and she watches* JIM *as he demonstrates the Australian crawl.*)

Now the coordination has to come from knowing how to synchronize the speed. The rate of speed that your feet are taking has to match that of your stroking speed. The reason you can't put the two together is because you're not concentrating on the whole mechanism. That is, you're becoming more concerned with one end or the other rather than the collaboration of the two as a total unit.

MAID. I see.

JIM. Now start out slowly, keeping that in mind.

(*She starts doing the crawl,* JIM *watches her for a while, then starts doing it himself.*)

Keep it slow, trying to work on the points where you derive the most power. Think of the way an oar or a paddle is constructed. Regard your arms and legs as being paddles. A paddle has a broad surface and reaches its highest point of thrust when it is perpendicular to the surface line of the water. This is the way you should use your arms. Keep your fingers close together to make a broader surface. Be careful not to let any water pass between them. That's it. Now the breathing is important. This requires added concentration and coordination. You will be able to breathe instinctively in the right manner if you keep in mind that the human being cannot inhale water.

MAID (*still doing the stroke*). Really?

JIM. Your head should pivot on your shoulders, always to the left. Inhale as your head comes out of the water and exhale as it goes into the water. Breathe in. Breathe out. In, out. In, out.

(*They both breathe and continue the stroking.*)

MAID. In, out. In, out.

JIM. One, two. One, two. That's right. Remember the whole thing is working at once.

MAID. I'm getting tired.

JIM. It's no sweat. Keep it up. You can't poop out in the middle of a lake. Stroke! Stroke! Keep it moving. One, two. One, two. Atta girl.

MAID. It's my back. There's a pain in my back.

(*She continues to swim,* JIM *goes faster.*)

JIM. That's good. It's good when it hurts. It's working then. Keep it up! We've almost got it. Hup, two! Hup, two!

MAID. It really aches, Jim.

JIM. That's all right. We're halfway already.

MAID. I'll never make it! My back.

JIM. Use it all. Everything at once. Make it work. One, two. One, two. (*He is going very fast with perfect coordination.*) In, out. In, out. Breathe! Breathe!

MAID. My leg! I've got a cramp, Jim! (*She continues very slowly.*)

JIM. Hup, two! Hup, two! Shake it off. Use it! Keep using it so it doesn't tighten. Keep it loose! Hup, two! Hup, two!

MAID. My side now! It's in my side!

JIM. Move it! Work it out! Keep it up!

MAID. Oh my leg! I can't! I can't do it! (*She continues slowly.*) It's killing me!

JIM. We're almost there!

(*The* MAID *screams in agony, she lies very still on the bed with her face in the blanket,* JIM *stops and looks at her, he sits on the edge of the bed.*) Did you drown, maidy?

(*She remains very still.*)

Did maidy drown in the middle of the lake? Tsk, tsk, tsk, tsk.

MAID. I got a cramp.

JIM. A leg cramp and a side cramp. What a shame.

MAID. It's not very funny.

JIM. I guess we can't go then, right?

MAID. Go where?

JIM. Swimming. At night. Night swimming. Swimming in the dark in the middle of the forest. Like we wanted to do. Remember?

MAID. We could if you'd take it slower. If you wouldn't rush. How can I learn all that in one sitting? In, out. In, out. Breathe! Breathe! You can make it! I'm not an advanced swimmer, you know. I'm a beginner. I know nothing about swimming and suddenly I'm supposed to have everything under my belt. Just intuitively I'm supposed to. It's pretty unfair, Jim.

JIM. I know.

MAID. If I get a cramp, I get a cramp. I can't go plodding on like an Olympic champion or something. Jesus Christ.

JIM. I'm sorry.

MAID. It takes time to be a swimmer.

(*She sits up on the bed.* JIM *remains where he is.*) I can't just become a swimmer in one lesson like that. I mean what is that? There's no water or anything and you expect me to swim! How can I swim on a bed! How can I do it!

JIM. I don't know.

MAID. I don't know either. I really don't. I can see me in a lake. Can you imagine me in a lake in the middle of the night with nobody around? Me and you in the middle of the forest, in the middle of a lake. And there you are, fifty yards ahead of me yelling: "In, out! In, out! You can make it! You can make it! Keep it up!" (*She stands and crosses down center, limping and holding her side.*) And I'm sinking fifty yards behind you. That's what I'd be doing, you know. Do you know that! I'd be sinking!

JIM. Yes.

MAID. Yes. The maid is slowly sinking. Gurgling, yelling, floundering for help. Sinking to the bottom of the lake on her first swimming lesson. Her first time out.

JIM.   Well take it easy. It's not my fault.

(*The* MAID *limps more deliberately and holds her side in mock agony.*)

MAID.   The maid bobbing up and down, up and down with her hands slapping the water, her mouth gasping for air, her side screaming with pain.

JIM.   I thought you'd swam before.

MAID.   Wading is what I did before! Tiptoeing in shallow water with my sneakers on! Not in seventy-five feet of lake water with no one around. Stranded there at night with my family in town and me in the forest and you wandering around smoking cigarettes in a tree and not giving a damn at all!

(JIM *stands and crosses to the* MAID.)

JIM.   Try to keep it moving. Work it out.

MAID.   I can't now. It's cramped for good. I'll never swim again.

JIM.   I know but keep it going. Keep the blood moving.

MAID.   It'll never work. The pain is unbelievable.

JIM.   Come on. Hup, two! Hup, two! You can make it.

MAID.   Nobody able to eat at home because I'm drowning out here! Nobody knowing where I am. Everybody forgetting my name! And I'm getting worse all the time! I'm sinking more and more! With seaweed up my nose and tangled all around me and I can't see a thing in the night!

(*She sinks to her knees and starts crawling around the stage on all fours as* JIM *follows her.*)

JIM.   Will you please cut it out.

MAID.   So you don't like me screaming out here, is that it? You don't like me getting carried away with my cramps and my pain in the middle of the night, in the middle of the forest. Well let me tell you it hurts me to do it. I don't like screaming myself. I try to keep a calm house, an easy home with everyone quiet and happy. It's not an easy thing, Jim. At my age, in my condition.

JIM.   Get up off the floor.

MAID. I make the beds and cook the meals. Everyone gets fed on time at my house.

JIM. I don't care. It's six o'clock now!

MAID. So the screaming shouldn't hurt you at all, knowing I don't do it all the time. Knowing that I save it for special times when my side starts to ache and my legs collapse and the water gets into my nose.

JIM. We can get you a doctor but you have to get up.

(*She collapses on the floor and stays very still with* JIM *standing over her.*)

Come on. I'll take you into town.

MAID. But once it's over it isn't bad at all. Once you get over the shock of having water all around and dragon-flies and water lilies floating by and little silver fish flashing around you. Once that's past and you get all used to your flippers and your fins and your new skin, then it comes very easy. (*She stands slowly with no concern at all for her cramps and gathers together all the dirty laundry as she continues to talk.*) You move through the water like you were born in that very same place and never even knew what land was like. You dive and float and sometimes rest on the bank and maybe chew on some watercress. And the family in town forgets where you went and the swimming coach forgets who you are and *you* forget all about swimming lessons and just swim without knowing how and before you know it the winter has come and the lake has frozen and you sit on the bank staring at the ice. You don't move at all. You just sit very still staring at the ice until you don't feel a thing. Until your flippers freeze to the ground and your tail freezes to the grass and you stay like that for a very long time until summer comes around.

(*She glances at* JIM *and then exits out the door with the linen;* JIM *stares after her for a second, then rushes toward the door.*)

JIM. Hey! I could drive you home! (*He opens the door and looks out.*) Hey! Do you want a lift!

(*He shuts the door, then turns downstage; he pauses, then rushes to his pants, he starts to put his pants on hurriedly, he gets them halfway on and* CAROL *enters, she is carrying a bag of groceries and wearing glasses, the door slams behind her,* JIM *looks at her for a second, then finishes putting on his pants,* CAROL *sets the groceries down on the stage left bed.*)

CAROL. Well. Guess what. A funny little thing. A very funny thing. I'm in the grocery store, see. I'm standing there looking for bread or something and guess what?

JIM. What?

CAROL. I start itching.

(*She crosses down right;* JIM *stands center with his back to the audience, staring at the door.*)

Not just a simple itch but a burn. A soaring kind of thing. A biting, scratching thing that's tearing at me, see.

(JIM *crosses slowly upstage and stands looking out the screen door.*)

Well I'm paralyzed. I don't know what to do because it's all up my legs and under my arms. (*She walks back and forth downstage.*) I can't start scratching my private zones right in the middle of a grocery store. So I run to the bathroom. I make a beeline for the bathroom and I lock the door and I rip my clothes off. I literally tear them off my body. And I look. And do you know what it is? Bugs! Bugs all over me. Buried in my skin. Little tiny itty bitty bugs, clawing and biting at me. They're all in my hair and everything. Sucking my blood, Jim! They're actually in my skin. I've been carrying them around with me. And do you know what? I have a sneaking suspicion that they're in this room. I picked them up from being in this room. I'll bet they're right inside here. In the beds even. (*She goes to the stage right bed and rips off the bedspread and the sheets.*) They're breeding in those beds. I'll bet you any amount of money. These cabins are so old and filthy. I bet they've been here for years without anybody checking. Bedbugs are no joke, Jim. I mean they suck your blood and everything. (*She goes to the other bed and tears it apart.*) I can't stand it. Just thinking about it upsets me. We'll have to get another room. That's all there is to it. Either that or go back home. I really can't take it. It's awful. Jim!

(JIM *turns to her slowly, there is a stream of blood running down his forehead.*)

JIM. What?
CAROL. What happened!
JIM. When?
  (*Blackout.*)

SAND
Murray Mednick

Playbill for Premiere Production

SAND

by Murray Mednick

Presented at Theatre Genesis
(St. Mark's Church-in-the-Bouwerie, New York City)

Directed by Ralph Cook

CAST

THE MOTHER ....Jean Granirer

THE FATHER ....Sully Boyar

THE AMBASSADOR ....David Scott Milton

1st SOLDIER ....Glenn Johnson

2nd SOLDIER ....Sam Black

Setting and lighting design: Kit Jones
Technical director: Kit Jones
Stage manager: Sheila Ferrini

Notes to any future production:

Lighting should emphasize the isolation of the characters from one another. THE AMBASSADOR never looks or speaks directly to anybody; he is always "on camera." In the opening section of the play, there are long pauses between each of the speeches, which grow smaller and smaller until the entrance of THE AMBASSADOR. The Offstage Voice should seem to emanate from the television set, if this is possible. All entrances and exits are made through an area of darkness backstage. A hum from an oscillator is heard throughout.

M.M.

MURRAY MEDNICK

"I'm the best tambourine player in Boo City. That were no easy pile a shit. I can make a cobra wiggle its ass & eat a hot dog.

"America should be run by the Chief of the Sioux. Who would know better how you don't scratch leave it alone? You'd get your money's worth. Turn everybody loose. Save your napalm for Plutonian Steam Heat.

"My friends are watching me. Cosmic Paranoia Drives My Car. Since I can remember there's been a war on.

"I was an ace Mountain Rat. I could carry 24 Main Dishes from the Kitchen to the Dining Room. I quit."

CHARACTERS

THE MOTHER: in her early forties, run down, wearing a dirty housecoat.

THE FATHER: late forties, fixated, but still vigorous. He wears an undershirt, baggy pants, and slippers.

THE AMBASSADOR: fifty-five or so, grey, W.A.S.P. type formally dressed in the usual Ambassadorial attire.

THE SOLDIERS: disheveled, war-weary degenerates with Brooklyn accents.

THE SCENE: STAGE RIGHT, a large worn out sand-box. In it are some sticks and stones, a little sand, a few bottle caps, pieces of glass . . . STAGE LEFT, a toilet bowl mounted on a small platform. Between the sandbox and the commode, UPSTAGE, is an old armchair. The stage is raked.

An electrical, buzzing noise, just audible and constant, an oscillator noise.

Also, a television set, image flickering but the sound off, is situated to the rear of the house, behind the audience, and is plainly visible to the actors.

The MOTHER sits in the sandbox, playing in a desultory manner with the things there. The FATHER works the toilet bowl with a plumber's helper. The two are oriented by these activities throughout. There is a considerable pause before the MOTHER speaks.

MOTHER.   I can't wait 'til your son gets here. I can't wait. He'll fix you—you'll see!

FATHER.   He ain't no son of mine.

MOTHER.   Whose is he, then?

FATHER.   Yours.

MOTHER.   You had nothing to do with it, I suppose?

FATHER.   Could've been anybody. Didn't have to be me. It's a big hole. Could've been a dog . . . Or a telephone pole . . . For all I know.

MOTHER.   Shit! I haven't been out of your sight long enough to get wet!

FATHER.   So big, the only thing I remember is the fear of drowning in it.

MOTHER.   Not even a little wet . . . *(Remembers.)* It tickled.

FATHER.   Swore I'd never go back in there. *(Plunges harder.)* And I never will! Never! Never! Never!

MOTHER.   Well who invited you, anyway? You stink!

104

FATHER (*struck*). A troll! A troll invited me! (*He laughs at her.*)

MOTHER. Oh I hope he kicks you down the stairs!

FATHER. Who? Who will?

MOTHER. Your son!

FATHER. Hah . . . You know what a troll is? . . . Huh? . . . You know what a troll is? . . . It's a bug! . . . It's a big bug on its hind legs . . . That's right!

MOTHER. I hope he stomps on you.

FATHER. Yes!—That was one time too many! Never again! (*Threatening with plunger.*) I'm on my guard!

MOTHER. And you better let him go to the bathroom! He's my only child!

FATHER. O no! He'll have to pay! Like everyone else!

MOTHER. That's not fair!

FATHER. Who does he think he is? It's MY fuckin' latrine! That's all there is to it!

MOTHER. What if he has to do a No. 2 in the middle of the night?

FATHER. O no! O no! The more he contributes, the harder I have to work. He'll have to go next door and use theirs.

MOTHER. They're liable to kill him . . . if he does a No. 2 in their latrine . . . in the middle of the night . . . They might kill him!

FATHER. That's his problem, not mine.

MOTHER. My God! Twenty years I've spent with you! Twenty years!

FATHER. Shut up! How many times have I told you to stop bothering me when I'm working?

MOTHER. You call that work?

FATHER. Are you kidding? Are you kidding? Do you think this is easy? Do you think this is pleasant?

MOTHER. It's smelly and boring.

FATHER. Look who's talking! Look at you—diddling yourself all day long!

MOTHER. I am not diddling myself! I'm trying to concentrate! I'm trying to think! But you—you've got shit on the mind! It's a disease!

FATHER. Someone has got to do it. Someone has got to get this thing cleared up! I've got to unclog this system once and for all!

MOTHER. It'll be clogged up until you croak. You're doomed!

FATHER. Quiet! (*A pause. He listens. Observes* M.) That's right . . . you make me think of trolls . . . Trolls and flushing water . . . that's right . . . God knows where your son came from!

MOTHER. He's YOUR responsibility! He comes from you!

(*A knock at the door. They don't hear it.*)

FATHER. Quiet! Damn you, I'll flush you down here one of these days!

(*Another knock.*)

MOTHER. I dare you!

(*She throws a bottle cap at him. He threatens with the plunger. The* AMBASSADOR *knocks and enters. A silence.*)

AMBASSADOR. How do you do? May I come in?

(*They scrutinize him. He hesitantly steps forward.*)

MOTHER. You're already in.

AMBASSADOR. Yes. Well . . . I am the Ambassador.

FATHER. Ambassador what?

AMBASSADOR. The Ambassador . . . Yes. From the Embassy.

FATHER (*sarcastic*). No shit?

AMBASSADOR. Yes. Well. I am afraid I have some bad news.

MOTHER. I'm not surprised. What else do we get around here.

AMBASSADOR. Oh? Well . . . It concerns your son—

FATHER. It's HER son. I'm not responsible . . . What did he do now?

AMBASSADOR. Missing in action.

FATHER. "Missing in action"? What kind of action?

MOTHER. The wrong kind, obviously.

FATHER. In Brooklyn?

AMBASSADOR. I'm terribly sorry—that's classified information.

MOTHER. What?—are you high class or something?

AMBASSADOR (*flustered*). Yes . . . Uh, not exactly. I did graduate . . .

MOTHER (*to* A.). Fuck you.

AMBASSADOR. In the top ten . . .

FATHER (*to* M.). Idiot!

MOTHER (*to* F.). Fuck you, too!

AMBASSADOR (*dignified*). I am a civil servant . . .

FATHER (*to* M.). Twenty years ago I thought you'd bury yourself in that stuff. I'm still waiting!

MOTHER (*shouting*). I've told you over and over! I don't have enough sand! I don't have enough sand! I need more sand! Why don't you get a job?

FATHER (*winking at* A.). Because I'm a very busy man, that's why. I have important obligations.

MOTHER (*sorrowfully*). There just isn't enough . . .

AMBASSADOR. Please . . . If I may have your attention a moment . . .

MOTHER. To go around . . . Is there?

AMBASSADOR (*pulling himself together*). Well . . .

MOTHER (*sure now*). Is there?

AMBASSADOR. Yes, of course . . . You see, sand is needed by the complex.

MOTHER. By the complex . . . ?

AMBASSADOR. Yes. It is mixed with chemicals . . .

FATHER. Water!

AMBASSADOR. Yes, water . . . To make . . .

MOTHER. Concrete.

AMBASSADOR. Yes. Concrete.

FATHER (*to* M.). Very good. You pass. You may go on to the third grade.

MOTHER. That's why . . .

AMBASSADOR (*almost whispering*). Yes.

MOTHER. There's a shortage!

AMBASSADOR. Yes.

(*A pause. She thinks.* F. *stops plunging and watches her.* A. *is distracted.*)

MOTHER. Concrete . . .

AMBASSADOR. Yes . . . Uh . . . May I sit down?

FATHER (*to* A.). How come you say "yes" all the time?

AMBASSADOR. What?

(F. *plunges.* M. *points and laughs at him.*)

MOTHER. Shmuck!

FATHER (*to* M.). Shut up! (*To* A.) Sit down.

AMBASSADOR. Yes . . . (*Pause. Sits. Resumes.*) The

complex needs a great deal of cement. *(Pause.)* A great deal. *(Sighs.)* To fill in all the holes, you understand . . .

FATHER. What holes?

AMBASSADOR. Yes. Holes. Everywhere. So many holes to fill. *(Sighs.)* So many. *(Pause.)* Holes.

MOTHER *(coming to life)*. Maybe I'll do that, Daddy.

FATHER. Don't call me "Daddy"!

MOTHER *(concentrating)*. I'll make it into concrete and I'll sell it to the complex.

FATHER. You can't.

MOTHER. Why can't I?

FATHER. You don't have the right chemicals. You need chemicals. Give it up.

MOTHER *(shouting)*. Water! I need water!

FATHER. And chemicals! *(To A.)* Right?

AMBASSADOR. Yes. Some.

MOTHER. What chemicals!?

AMBASSADOR. Yes. Well . . . That is to say . . .

MOTHER *(shouting)*. Get me some chemicals!

FATHER. I don't know which ones they are, stupid!

MOTHER. Get them from him! He's an Ambassador!

AMBASSADOR *(firmly)*. I'm afraid that's impossible.

FATHER. Besides, I'm occupied at the moment.

MOTHER. And some goddamned water!

AMBASSADOR. May I—?

FATHER. You know we can't spare any water! What's the matter with you? I use water in my work! You know that! Without water—it's incredible! . . . It won't go down!

(Again she points and laughs. A pause.)

FATHER. I know where there's one big old hole for you to fill, Ambassador.

AMBASSADOR. Yes! Everywhere! In all directions! And yet—it must be done. And we are the ones who have to do it.

MOTHER *(to F.)*. Excuses! All I get from you is excuses! You're just not big enough!

FATHER. It's gigantic, Ambassador. Believe me. A cavern is what it is. A cavern! With a huge lake at the bottom of it.

MOTHER. See—he's afraid of drowning. He admitted it!

AMBASSADOR. Ah, yes, a common affliction . . . heh, heh, like the cold . . . Uh, unfortunately, we've none to spare. Nothing at all. Nevertheless, we MUST take care of it, of course. A continent at a time, to be sure. But we MUST take responsibility for the filling of holes.

> (F. *and* M. *have ceased their activities and are staring at him. A pause. He grows discomfited*).

Yes . . . A single continent . . . Now, to arrive at the point of this . . . visit . . .

MOTHER. The point?

FATHER. What's on your mind, Ambassador?

AMBASSADOR (*to* M.). Yes. About your son . . .

MOTHER. MY son! It's his, too!

FATHER. Impossible! He never could've made the distance!

MOTHER. What distance?

FATHER (*gesturing*). Up. The distance UP.

AMBASSADOR. I beg your pardon?

FATHER (*dreamily*). Upstream all the way . . .

MOTHER (*to* A.). Do you know what he did? He tried to flush him down there once! That's right! A little boy! He said our SON was clogging the system!

FATHER. He was!

MOTHER. It's been a hassle from the beginning, Ambassador. It's been no picnic living with that man.

AMBASSADOR (*embarrassed*). Oh? Well, these are difficult times . . . For the youth especially . . . The nation's youth is quite confused . . .

MOTHER. Right from the start, he wasn't safe. My little boy! I had to keep a constant lookout—for him! (*Pointing at* F.) I had to watch him every step of the way! My boy and I! We stuck together! We took our nap. We went to the bathroom. We had to! We went to bed . . . on time! My boy and I! We took care of each other! I made sure . . . I kept him nice and clean . . . I wiped his ass . . .

FATHER (*shaking plunger*). I caught him! I caught him in the act! Red-handed!

AMBASSADOR. Yes.

FATHER. Yes—what?

AMBASSADOR. Your son. Caught, probably.

MOTHER (*dazed*). They caught him.

AMBASSADOR (*sighing*). Yes.

> (*A silence.*)

Of course, we could trade for him. If we knew.

MOTHER. You don't know?

(*A silence.*)

FATHER. I think you're full of shit. That's what I think.

AMBASSADOR. I beg your pardon?

MOTHER. He thinks everything is full of shit.

FATHER. Everything is! Ask him!

AMBASSADOR. Well . . . I wouldn't put it that way . . . Ahem . . . Various interpretations of the situation. (*Pause.*) In any case, there are two alternatives—trade, or pay.

FATHER. The drainage system must be improved all around! And the pipes! The pipes must be cleaned out immediately! For Christ's sake! They oughta take one of them flamethrowers and blow all that shit out of the pipes! Miles and miles of shitty pipes! For Christ's sake!

MOTHER. The Ambassador is trying to tell us something . . . Aren't you, Ambassador?

AMBASSADOR. Yes . . . We must now use the term "Revolutionary Development."

(*A silence.*)

FATHER. He's a communist!

AMBASSADOR (*chuckling*). No, no. No, no. I mean, simply, that the phrase—"Revolutionary Development"— is to be preferred to the former term . . . "Pacification" . . . which described the very same . . . process . . . of course.

MOTHER. Of course.

FATHER. I don't care what you call it! It's all the same shit to me!

MOTHER. Naturally . . . But that's interesting, Ambassador . . . ?

AMBASSADOR. Well, yes. Yes.

FATHER (*plunging furiously*). Yes! Yes! Yes! Yes! Yes!

MOTHER (*to A.*). He's out of his mind.

FATHER. Yes! Yes! Yes! Yes! (*Stops abruptly.*) Let me tell you about that hole of hers, Ambassador. It's . . . (*He makes a picture with his hands, at a loss for words.*) it's . . . a revolutionary development!

AMBASSADOR. Precisely.

MOTHER (*amazed*). My, My. Holy mother of Jesus!

FATHER (*winking*). You think you could fill that hole, Ambassador? Heh, heh.

AMBASSADOR (*subsiding*). Yes. Oh. Well. That is to say—All the holes will be filled. In due time. According to plan. I am myself . . . I am a civil servant. Nevertheless, the former term is to be discarded, and the new one is to be employed.

MOTHER (*flirtatious*). No question about it. There's no question about it. Not to my mind. That's fascinating, Ambassador.

FATHER. Heh, heh.

MOTHER. Him, of course, you might as well forget. He doesn't think much.

FATHER (*giggling*). Heh, heh. I'd really like to see that. Ha! I really would like to see that.

AMBASSADOR. Well . . . Not all at once. Perhaps a continent, a single continent . . . at a time. It will take years! Decades! But we are acting from strength! We are marshalling our forces! Our sand! Our water! Our precious natural resources! So that one day . . . One day the entire planet will gleam like a fresh new highway in the rain! A shining, happy star! (*He leaps to his feet.*) Peace on earth! The Second Coming!

MOTHER (*clutching her breast*). My O my! God help me!

FATHER (*plunging harder*). Yes, indeed. I want to be there for that one, allright! I want to be alive for that one.

AMBASSADOR (*coming to his senses*). Thirty-three dollars and ninety cents a body is the current rate of exchange. Thirty-three dollars and ninety cents . . .

(*Everything stops. A silence.*)

MOTHER. What did you say?

FATHER. He said the going rate is thirty-three dollars and ninety cents a body. Heh, heh.

MOTHER (*indignant*). WHOSE body?

FATHER. That's the going rate, eh? More than it's worth, heh, heh. (*To M.*) You ought to take it before the price goes down.

AMBASSADOR. No. You don't understand. You see—a given number is unavoidably sacrificed. A fraction of the population. There's no help for it. Of necessity . . .

MOTHER. I resent that! I truly resent that!

FATHER. Prices are bound to fall. That's the way it goes.

AMBASSADOR. Trade, or pay . . . Trade, or pay . . .

(*A silence.* M. *and* F. *observe* A.)

That is to say . . . The missing body . . .

VOICE ON TAPE. We have FOUND the body.

AMBASSADOR. Yes.

(F. *clears throat, plunges madly.* M. *gazes at* A. *Gazes, shifts.*)

FATHER. What the fuck! What the fuck!

(A. *takes out rumpled piece of paper, writes.*)

AMBASSADOR. I must revise my previous statement.

FATHER. Ah, the hell with it!

AMBASSADOR (*putting it away*). Perhaps I should explain . . .

MOTHER (*fixedly*). You should get me some water at least. At least some goddamned water.

FATHER (*by rote*). I've told you a million times—no noise. No noise.

AMBASSADOR. If, for example, a suit is brought against us—

FATHER. A million times!

AMBASSADOR. —we must pay . . . For one of them—

MOTHER. I just don't understand it.

AMBASSADOR. —at the rate of thirty-three dollars and ninety cents a body—

FATHER. That's too high! That sounds too high to me! It's inflationary!

AMBASSADOR. —to the family of the deceased.

FATHER. It's inflationary!

MOTHER (*aloud to herself*). Never enough. There's never enough. I don't understand it. (*To* F.) Just get the money, will you?

AMBASSADOR. For one of them, as I say, if it is a civilian. As the case may be.

FATHER. How about one of us? US?

AMBASSADOR. Yes. Well, it costs us two hundred and fifty thousand dollars to kill one real guerilla. Those are the latest figures.

MOTHER (*intensely frustrated, almost crying*). Why can't we hear it? Why can't you turn it up?

AMBASSADOR. It's quite complicated, as you can see. It's not clear-cut. Not at all. There are: insurance plans . . . Defoliation . . . Graduated income . . . Revolutionary development . . .

FATHER. Too much noise!

AMBASSADOR. I should say, however, that one of ours is worth five of theirs! Five times as much. A five to one ratio. That comes to one hundred and eighty-five dollars.

FATHER. I don't get it. Something's wrong there.

AMBASSADOR. Things change. The pressure of events, the balance of payments et cetera.

FATHER. What about the two hundred and fifty thou?

MOTHER (*to herself*). Sand is expensive.

AMBASSADOR (*encouraged*). Yes. Now, exchanges are possible—in certain situations. Depending on the terrain, the conditions, the price, as well as other, equally unpredictable . . . contingencies.

FATHER. Hmm. We've GOT to go easy on the moisture supply!

MOTHER. Water, water, water, water . . . Why don't you DO something?

FATHER. Do something? . . . I'm DOING SOMETHING!

AMBASSADOR. In this particular . . . instance . . . that concerning your son . . .

MOTHER (*by rote*). My son! my son!

AMBASSADOR. Yes.

FATHER. What the fuck?

AMBASSADOR (*matter of fact*). History presses down on us. Craters proliferate. Proliferate. They must be filled up. We must hold the line. Times are hard.

(F. *plunges ferociously, muttering.*)

MOTHER (*sad, sifting twigs, etc.*). A shortage of sand?

AMBASSADOR. Whenever possible, a habeas corpus is to be preferred above the other, less fiscally sound, alternatives.

VOICE ON TAPE. You may have the body.

AMBASSADOR. Yes.

MOTHER (*to* F.). Can't you turn it up? Please! Can't you turn it up?

FATHER. Too much noise! Too much goddamned noise!

MOTHER. I don't understand. I just—

AMBASSADOR. We try to deliver. We keep our word. We save face. We honor our commitments.

FATHER (*plunging away*). Yes—Yes—Yes—Yes—!

AMBASSADOR. We are moving forward. We are flexible. We are reliable and rich. We are viable. We are voracious. We have an appetite—

FATHER. YES —yes—yes—yes—yes!

AMBASSADOR. —We fill the holes. We create a free and solid order among men. A grey, concrete, secure . . . temple! Freedom! Founded on goodwill, on a universal respect for cement! For the hard economic facts!

FATHER. Yes! —Yes! —Yes! —Yes!

MOTHER (*deranged*). STOP! PLEASE!

(*A long pause. F. and A. regard M.*)

My . . .? It's so cold . . . I just don't understand it . . . (*Shivers.*) My . . . ? Silently flickering . . . (*Shivers.*) Always silently flickering . . . (*She stares steadily back at* A.)

AMBASSADOR. I'm sorry.

FATHER. Ha! I think it's going down! It's going down!

MOTHER (*by rote*). Go down! Go down with it!

AMBASSADOR. You seem extremely . . . This is very difficult . . .

FATHER (*shouting*). Forget it! Forget it!

MOTHER. Vile. Vile air. Vile talk. So thick you can hardly breathe. (*She breathes into cupped hands.*) Bad breath by the millions. Can't understand it . . . Never get through the muck! Millions!

FATHER (*muttering*). Never quite makes it . . . The shit will not go down . . .

AMBASSADOR. Nevertheless, I have heavy duties. Yes. Burdens. (*Looks at watch.*) Time is running out. Your son . . .

FATHER. Shit!

MOTHER (*to* A.). I don't know what you're talking about. What are you talking about?

VOICE ON TAPE. Ambassador! Here is the body, Ambassador!

AMBASSADOR. Yes. We keep score, you know. Not always accurate, of course . . . Due to the constant un-

known. The probabilities. Something like that . . . Yes,
we do count—you can bet on it.

MOTHER (*to* F.). Did you hear it?

(*A pause.* F. *cocks ear and observes* A., *who has
taken out a checkbook and is writing in it. We
hear the sounds of wheels and pulleys offstage. The
TWO SOLDIERS enter with a young corpse in uniform. The bloodied corpse is hung on a large meat-
hook, which is attached by a chain to a pipe overhead. The soldiers maneuver it to CENTER STAGE
where it slowly revolves.*)

AMBASSADOR. One hundred and eighty-five dollars and
. . . no cents.

1st SOLDIER. Phew! What a stench!

2nd SOLDIER. I can't stand it anymore!

MOTHER (*like a frustrated child*). No! No! No!

FATHER. Shut up! Shut up!

(AMBASSADOR *rises, tears off check, sighs, holds
breath, places check in vestpocket of corpse. Com-
poses himself, nods to* F., *takes a step toward*
MOTHER.)

AMBASSADOR. Thank you so much. You have been
most cooperative. I am terribly sorry. Goodbye. (AM-
BASSADOR *bows, exits.* 2nd SOLDIER *does the Up Yours
with his arm, spits into sandbox.*)

2nd SOLDIER. I've got to get away from this stink!
It's all over me!

1st SOLDIER. You need a hot bath, that's all.

MOTHER (*softly*). I held his hand. I wiped his ass.

FATHER (*fierce whisper*). Shut up! Shut up!

(1st SOLDIER *approaches* F. *and toilet bowl as* FATHER
cringes.)

1st SOLDIER. Move out, Daddy! Move! Move!

(*He throws* FATHER *to his knees and takes a piss as*
2nd SOLDIER *discovers blood on his hands.*)

2nd SOLDIER. Damn! Look at this!

(*He tries wiping hands on corpse's uniform.*)
Fucking meat!

(*He turns, goes to sandbox where* MOTHER *is rocking to and fro with her head in her hands. He
picks up handful of sand, dirt, etc. and rubs his
hands briskly, then lingers a moment.*)

1st SOLDIER (*buttoning up*). What are you waiting for? Let's get out of here.

(*Pause.*)

Come on, Man. She's all dried up. You couldn't get into that with an ax.

2nd SOLDIER (*rubbing his hands*). Yeah, let's get out of here.

(*They exit.*)

(*A long pause.* FATHER *rises. They watch the corpse a moment, then turn away.*)

MOTHER. Why don't you turn it up? I can't hear it. Why don't you turn it up?

FATHER (*plunging again, through clenched teeth*). I've told you a million times! Too much noise! Too much goddamned noise!

(*A pause. Blackout.*)

FRUIT SALAD

Grant Duay

Playbill for Premiere Production

FRUIT SALAD
by Grant Duay

Presented at Theatre Genesis
(St. Mark's Church-in-the-Bouwerie, New York City)

Directed by Tony Barsha

CAST

BANANA ....Beeson Carroll

MELON ....Nick Orzel

CHERRY ....Randall Bane

Music: Elliot Kaplan
Film: Tony Barsha
Photography: Stanton Kaye
Assistant: Nino Infante
Scenic artist: Bob Burke
Lighting design: Kit Jones
Costumes: Sonia Nolff
Technical director: Kit Jones
Stage manager: Sheila Ferrini
Electrician: Ronnie Smtak
Projectionists: Pat Sheen, Jim Rawlins
Production assistant: Margit Winckler

GRANT DUAY

"I was born in New Jersey, attended schools in Newark and Cranford and majored in Journalism at Miami University.

"I began writing screenplays three years ago during which time I received invaluable experience in different phases of film making, working on underground short films and pilot TV commercials. *Fruit Salad* is my first play.

"At present, I'm reworking my previously written screenplays, transferring them to other mediums."

(Editor's note: This is a live play with intermittently simultaneous film in which the filmed episodes are summarized in a position with relation to the printed script which simulates the stage-to-screen juxtaposition.)

(*Scene: The locale of the play is the jungle during war-time and it is night. There are no sets.*

A vertical movie screen is mounted centrally up stage.

Organist enters, sits at organ console up right, turns light on and puts sheet music on rack and plays prelude. Begins slightly ecclesiastical, changes to ominous (house lights slowly dim to off) and reaches a dramatic climax, dissolves to single penetrating note . . . changing to a perky light bridge . . . Orchestra plays a perky light bridge and frivolous theme which changes to sweeping carefree waltz.

FILM: *On screen up center, we see flashing colors . . . A young charming girl stands before table and selects the Banana from a bunch, the Melon from several and the Cherry from a jar of many. She places each fruit on cutting board and moves clear glass bowl onto cutting board and stands smiling at audience . . . flashing colors. The film is photographed in saccharine colors giving effect of TV commercial. Carefree waltz ceases. We see small green lights on periphery of stage and hear distant machine gun fire . . . a thundering jet plane passes overhead . . . distant gun fire . . . loud burst of machine gun fire.*

BANANA, MELON *and* CHERRY *run to center stage, diving onto floor.* BANANA *wears bright yellow coveralls.* MELON *wears green coveralls and* CHERRY *wears hot red coveralls. They all wear silver helmets and white sneakers. Each carries a child's gold painted plastic rifle which is dotted with red sequins. They keep down as bullets pass overhead.* BANANA *starts to get up, ready to run.* MELON *pulls him down.)*

MELON. Stay down! You want to get killed?

BANANA. We're pinned! They got us trapped!

MELON. It's not hopeless. We'll get out of it! You'll get us out. Like before!

CHERRY. Hey, Lieutenant! What about the others—the Sergeant's group? They're up on the hill—we got to get to them!

MELON. And get chopped down by the enemy machine gun? To hell with the Sarge and his boys! Right, Banana?

BANANA. Yeah!

CHERRY. Listen, Banana! We gotta at least make an attempt. We gotta reach them! We'll have a better chance! We can all get out of this together. See what I mean?

BANANA. Right!

MELON. Cherry's shittin' in his pants! He can't think straight! He cares more for the others! What about your own skin, uhh?

CHERRY. I'm thinking about my skin when I care what happens to the others! Lieutenant? The Melon only knows how to think about himself! We'll never make it if we don't join them!

BANANA. Cherry's right! I got to think. Wait a minute!

MELON. Don't take all night! Cherry's suicidal! Think about this Banana! You! Are we going to risk our skins for that—that FAG Sergeant, and his boys up on the hill? For a fag? It's good to think of others when you're pretty sure of seeing tomorrow! It's a luxury. We can't afford it now! BANANA! Not for a faggot! You know that, Lieutenant!

BANANA. I certainly do! Everybody knows about that *fag* Sergeant! He's worse than those other old time Sergeants who stay in service because of the new boys— the young recruits coming in! All their free time is spent *faggin'* around! I don't know why they haven't gotten rid of him. He should be thrown out. He's a freakin' disgrace! I'm not getting chopped down for that FAG!!!

MELON. Good man, Lieutenant! Now you're thinking!

CHERRY. Don't you have a conscience? We can't let them be cut off. So what if the Sergeant is fagged! Who cares if he's faggin' the boys?

MELON. That's enough, Cherry! Shut your mouth! Banana's decided! We ain't joining the others! That's it! Now Lieutenant, we gotta figure out a way to vacate—without getting hit in the back by machine gun bullets. You know what I mean?

BANANA. Exactly, Corporal. One of us should knock out that machine gun nest with a hand grenade.

MELON. One of us should grenade that machine gun nest. You should, Lieutenant! You got the most experience! Banana got a star for throwing a grenade into an enemy rifle squad! You've told us about it many times! It was in the ravine! You're the best man for the job! Agree?

BANANA. I am the best! This won't take long! (*Exits, heading for enemy machine gun.*)

MELON. I think he'll make it! The Banana can throw a grenade. Anybody can! Even you!

CHERRY. And how can you desert the others?

MELON. Forget it! It's finished! In the past!

CHERRY. What a job you did on the Lieutenant. You scooped that one right off a stinking low vine!

MELON. What the hell you talking about, Cherry?

CHERRY. You know! The Banana was going to have us join the Sarge and the boys but you brought up that FAG business! You were desperate! The Banana Lieutenant *hates* faggots! He's told us often enough. So you went to work on him. You used his hate, for your own selfish ends!

MELON. Bull shit! You're sour, Cherry! And if you don't shut up . . .

(*Sound of explosion as* BANANA *destroys enemy nest.*) That's the Lieutenant! He got the machine gun! We can scram!

CHERRY. Wait for the Lieutenant!

MELON. He may have got it in the head. If he gets back I don't want you buggin' him with that bull shit! You hear? . . . Or else . . . We don't go around to-gether—when we get leaves! You know what I mean?

CHERRY. Yeah.

MELON. Good. Where the hell is he? (*Short pause.*) I hear something! Point your gun over there! Ready to shoot!

> (BANANA *enters running and dives onto floor joining* MELON *and* CHERRY.)

BANANA. I got 'em! There were three of them! They didn't know what happened!

CHERRY. We know.

MELON. We heard the grenade!

BANANA. Get ready to make a break! I gotta check the map! (*Pulls map from back pocket and looks at it.*) Yeah—Uhhh-huhhh! Yeah! We're heading for the mountains! Okay men, let's go! Now!

> (BANANA, MELON *and* CHERRY *stand up quickly and run up stage and exit. Lights are extinguished.*
>
> FILM: *We see flashing colors on screen up center. Orchestra plays perky light and bright frivolous theme . . . changes to sweeping carefree waltz . . . then perky theme repeated twice. Salad girl cuts Banana and puts pieces into glass bowl. She cuts Melon in half and scoops pieces with spoon, putting pieces into bowl. Girl cuts Cherry into tiny pieces and puts them into bowl. She looks up smiling . . . flashing colors. Area up center is lit. Jungle birds and distant guns are heard. Orchestra stops playing.*
>
> BANANA, CHERRY *and* MELON *enter up center, double-time marching in place and continue moving about stage with lights following.*)

We're in the clear!

MELON. You're right, Banana. They'll put a star on your chest, next to the other one. It didn't seem possible, but then I was with you when we slid out of the aquamarine ravine during monsoon! Too bad you missed it, Cherry!

CHERRY. Yeah! Too bad for you because where do you suppose Banana got his first star?

MELON. The aquamarine ravine!

CHERRY. Like hell, Melon. The maroon lagoon. That's where! Ain't that so, Lieutenant?

BANANA. Yes! Cherry knows history. The ravine was spikes, the lagoon was a meat grinder bastard! But right now we're in the delta! You wouldn't be making it to the mountains if I hadn't grenaded that machine gun nest in the fuchsia forest!

MELON. I don't care what happened at the maroon lagoon! You still should have gotten a star for the ravine!

(*A short pause as actors move down center, continuing marching in place.*)

CHERRY. What about the others? I don't think they made it.

MELON. Probably not. Just thank Banana you're still running. See, the Lieutenant figured none of us would have a chance if we all busted out of the area together. If we all had, none of us would be able to tell about it! What's the point of that?

(*Organist plays a slow implacable background which is in complete contrast with the double-time marching actors.*)

BANANA. Melon knows tactics . . . He'll make a good Sergeant someday! . . . What separates a Lieutenant from a Private? . . . Decisiveness! Using what you've been taught and what you've learned, always making decisions. Keeping aspects under consideration plus a little intuition for a successful ending! That's a Lieutenant!

(CHERRY, BANANA *and* MELON *move, double-time marching, to up stage right.*)

MELON. Let's stop for a rest. I feel like jerking off! Now that we've made it.

CHERRY. That's all that's on your mind?

BANANA. Plenty of time to make it later, Melon. Keep running!

MELON. The Lieutenant Banana is a great leader because he never takes unnecessary chances. He'd have us running to the mountains without a break, if it was possible. How many miles to the mountains, Banana?

BANANA. Enough! I can't tell for sure right now. But when we rest I'll check the map. If you haven't lost it, Cherry!

CHERRY. What do you mean? You've got it right there in your pocket! Anyhow, my feet are raw. Man, let's stop running soon, real soon!

MELON. Stop crying, Cherry. This ain't no kids' game! As soon as we stop for a break, you'll start moaning and bitching about the freakin' giant insects. At least you ain't staying in one place so they could eat you all over!

> (BANANA *and* MELON *move down center,* CHERRY *lags behind double-time marching up center.*)

BANANA.   Hey Cherry! How many cans of rations do you have?

CHERRY.   Only got two left.

MELON.   Two? Man, you're going to starve and I ain't giving you none of mine because I told you to go easy before! I only got enough for myself!

BANANA.   Relax, Cherry. The Melon will share his rations, when the time comes. I won't have to remind him who's the reason for his being still alive!

MELON.   Of course, Lieutenant, I was fooling around, plucking the Cherry. He worries a hell of a lot over a whole lot of nothing. He's just a kid. An unexposed Cherry, running with a shrewd Banana and a well seasoned Melon!

> (*Organist stops playing implacable background.*)

CHERRY.   You got a big head! You're the only one that's done anything! You killed this many, you got out of that trap, you were with Banana at the ravine! Big deal, haven't we allllll . . .

> (*Loud burst of machine gun, flashing strobe light as* CHERRY, *up stage center,* MELON *and* BANANA, *down stage center, fall to floor. They all freeze in darkness.*)

MELON.   HE'S HIT!!!

> (FILM: *Orchestra plays sweeping carefree waltz as flashing colors appear on film screen, up stage center. We see young pretty girl pouring orange, grape and cherry juices from various sized and shaped clear glass containers. She begins to stir fruit salad with large shiny spoon . . . flashing colors.*
>
> *Lights illuminate* BANANA *and* MELON, *down center.* BANANA *starts to get up but* MELON *pulls him down to floor.*)

Where the hell do you think you're going? Uhh?

BANANA.   Keep running! We can't stay here! They'll get us!

MELON. Easy Lieutenant! Relax man! You're all excited! Calm down. You're not running away. No! We get the Private! He's been hit. The Private ain't the others because he's one of us! Lieutenant? To hell with the others but the Private is us, he's we! Battle conditions are making you tense. You want to go all the way by yourself! I say no! We're getting the Private! You need me. We both need him—but right now he needs us most! Do you understand! Uhh?

BANANA. I forgot about him for a moment.

MELON. Some memory! What a rotten moment! Come on!

> (BANANA *and* MELON *crawl to wounded* CHERRY, *up stage center.* CHERRY's *area is lit. Occasional bursts of machine gun fire are heard.*)

BANANA. How bad is it?

MELON. It looks worse than it is. Shin bone splintered and he's bleeding a lot but this tourniquet will stop it. I think he's in shock! See if you have any stuff in your kit!

BANANA. Here it is.

MELON. Give it to him! Hurry! Cover that wound with antiseptic . . . I think they're all around us! What happened, Lieutenant?

BANANA. He'll be all right. Hey Private! It's nothing! Do you hear?

MELON. Yeah, he'll be all right but what about them? The enemy! What about us? Are we trapped again?

BANANA. That son of a bitch! Look at this insect bastard! Part of an advance force. We must keep killing these giant bastard insects, as fast as they come or they'll overrun us and what would the guys say about that? Getting finished by insects! Uh? Uh? Listen! You gotta fight back!!! You must kill them when they get too close! They're the enemy! You hear, man? Kill 'em!!

MELON. Sssssshhh! Quiet! I hear something! Come on! Over there!

> (MELON *and* BANANA *leave* CHERRY, *crawling to down center. They hold rifles in shooting position.* BANANA *prepares to shoot but* MELON *pulls* BANANA's *gun down.*)

Don't give away our position! We'll have to do plenty

of shooting in the morning—if we're still around! Are you
sure we're on our way to the mountains? We're trapped.
Moving in circles! Right, Banana?

BANANA. I'm going to check on the Private.

MELON. To hell with him! I want to know what's
up! What's going on? Why are we surrounded by the
enemy and how'd we get into this? Tell me why! You're
the leader, you're supposed to know!

BANANA. We're headed for the mountains. We gotta
dig in!

MELON. Where's the map? You had it last. I want to
check our position! Give it to me!

(BANANA *reaches into his pocket and pulls out map
and gives it to* MELON. *He looks at map thoroughly.*)

I know, you know how to read a map! You never looked
at it! LIEUTENANT!! A map is a guide. It tells you
where we are. What's inside your head? . . . Jesus Christ!
You know where we are? You really want to know?
We're here! Don't move, you might brush up against
one of them! Breathe softly, realize each breath, it
might be your last! Make friends with the insects! You
ain't got many and you need at least a few. Maybe by
morning you could have them all brainwashed and
disciplined for regimentation! They could attack the
enemy. And we would ooze out of here! Is that how we
got out of the ravine, Lieutenant? You must have some
extraordinary power, some weird force behind you . . .
because your brain is a fluffy downy!

BANANA. We have to dig in! Leave in the morning!

MELON. You said that before, stupid! What do you
think they'll do when they find us here? INFESTED!
They always have an investigation, you know that! And
they'll forget about your luck at the aquamarine ravine
and the maroon lagoon and they'll steal those stars, for
souvenirs. You better check on the Private. I'm taking
over! Scram fluffy! Scram! Move!

(BANANA *crawls over to wounded* CHERRY, *up stage
center.* MELON *stays on watch down stage center.*
MELON's *area is darkened.*)

You can explain it to him! How you bungled! This pre-
dicament is pretty hopeless and I've been through a lot
to know when things are dim.

(MELON'S *area is dimmed to dark.* BANANA *awakens*
CHERRY *up stage center.*

Organist plays implacable background.)

BANANA. Hey Private! Wake up. Talk to me.

CHERRY. What happened? Is that you, Lieutenant?

BANANA. Yes, it's me.

(FILM: *We see film on screen up center. Close-up of
fruit salad in bowl as pretty girl slowly stirs it.
Shots of* CHERRY *in student garb seated on bench
at quadrangle of Columbia University intercut with
shots of sinister heavyset cigar smoking man, who's
seated on same bench. Swish pans of university
buildings intercut with close-ups of bewildered*
CHERRY *and sinisterly smiling heavyset cigar smoking man. Camera zooms in on cross topped dome
of church and stops zoom showing part of church
dome without cross.*)

CHERRY. What happened?

BANANA. You got shot in the leg, but don't worry.
It was only a few stray bullets from some lost enemy
snipers. We're still going to the mountains but for now
we're digging in. We'll clear out in the morning.

CHERRY. Where's the Corporal? Is he all right?

BANANA. Yes! He's by himself, wants to be alone,
over there. I think he wants to jerk off!! You remember,
when we were running through the delta, that's what he
said he wanted to do!

CHERRY. I thought that was a joke. He must be crazy.

BANANA. He might be headin' that way but you know
the Corporal says what he means!

CHERRY. Why did I have to get shot up like this? I
thought we were in the clear!

BANANA. You got in the way of some sniper's bullets.
I already told you!

CHERRY. Nothing like this ever happened before when
you were leading. You always got us out without a
bruise. You sure there's only a few of them?

BANANA. Listen, Private—Private First Class! I haven't
failed you yet, have I? So just relax and we'll scram in
the morning, to the fresh air on the mountains! And
don't get upset if the Corporal starts shooting off his
mouth about our digging in here for the night. Because

I think this business is confusing him . . . he says crazy
things and you know the crazy thing he's doing right
now! Even you said so yourself!

CHERRY. I guess you're right.

BANANA. What do you mean *guess?* Who led you out
of the maroon lagoon? And the Corporal knows that it
was I who practically carried him out of the aquamarine
ravine! I grenaded the machine gun nest in the fuchsia
forest! That's why I can't understand why he's doubting
me and my proven judgment right now just because you
got hit by a few stray bullets!

CHERRY. It could be battle fatigue, right?

BANANA. They do get that way with fatigue, don't
they? Yeah. The purple paddy! That Sergeant! He cracked
up and started machine gunning the circling black vultures because they were picking the bones of the dead.
One guy hit him unconscious, because the enemy was
getting ready for an all out attack!

CHERRY. I hope the Corporal doesn't pull a stupid
act like that.

BANANA. Leave him alone, unless he gives a strong
indication. We need him! You don't think I'm able to
carry you out alone, do you?

CHERRY. And I don't want anything like that to
happen to him because—because—well, we've had a few
kicks, especially back in the city!

BANANA. You mean you went out to hunt for cunt?

CHERRY. We did everything.

BANANA. Oh yeah! Uhhh! Anyhow you and me will
go on a hunt when we get leaves, after we get to the
mountains. What do you say?

CHERRY. If my leg's healed and there's no complica-
tions. I just remembered! I made a deal to go looking
with the Corporal!

(*Organist stops playing.*)

BANANA. He won't be in any condition to go hunting, he needs treatment, a rest at the base maybe for a
month or two. Then he'll be a working Corporal again,
like he was before. A real good one! It's too bad this
had to happen to him right when we get leaves, but
they'll give him the best care! . . . How's your leg?

CHERRY. If I can walk we could clear out tonight.

BANANA. No! In the morning! We're digging in to-night, according to *my* plan!

MELON (*in darkness down center*). PLAN!!? What plan, crazy man? (*Walks up center joining* BANANA *and* CHERRY *and stands looking down at them.*)

CHERRY. Hey! You're talking to the Lieutenant! I've been telling him about the kicks we had back in the city!

MELON. That's great! But what's he been telling you? Uhhh? What's he been shittin' you with?

CHERRY. Are you crazy? He told me about this here Sergeant, the one back in the purple paddy.

BANANA. I told you not to talk to him!

MELON. You mean Sergeant Nobody, the imaginary somebody? Ha ha ha! What purple paddy?

BANANA. Don't argue with him! He's cracking up!

MELON. Why don't you tell him the truth, Lieutenant? Tell him there won't be a morning, for us! You blund-ered! I want you to tell him *everything* while I show him the *map!* The evidence!

(MELON *leans over showing map to* CHERRY. BANANA *stands angrily.*

FILM: *Film on screen up center shows close-up of fruit salad bowl as girl slowly stirs salad . . .* MELON, *wearing black leather jacket—dark pants, works on engine of car in street of lower middle-class New York neighborhood. Three similarly dressed friends appear.* MELON *and friends slouch on car and talk rapidly, gesticulate emphatically, joke and poke each other. They hide heads under hood of car, looking at engine. They then resume slouch positions and continue poking and joking.* MELON *moves car radio antenna up and down, then wipes hand on friend's leather jacket.* MELON's *leather pals leave him. He closes hood of car and walks toward camera in close-up with fire escaped buildings in background . . . Close-up of* MELON *looking up seriously.*)

BANANA. You're rotten, Corporal! You're out of your mind with poison! Lies!

(CHERRY *stands and they all move slowly about weaving circles.*)

CHERRY. The Corporal is fair! He knows what he can do and what he can't.

BANANA. To you, he would be that way. The Corporal and the Private go hunting together. They hang together on leaves and short free times off. Good times without the tension of battle conditions. You like the Corporal because he knows the way around. He's Corporal and you're only a Private First Class. But you only know the Corporal of leaves, short free times off, of the hunt and well scenes. There's another Corporal!

CHERRY. What do you mean?

MELON. He's crappin' you, Cherry!

BANANA. You're just a kid! What do you know? The half of it satisfies you. The rest doesn't exist. The Melon Myth has you deeper and deeper. *Cheap con artist yes and no man sir Melon!*

MELON. You're full of shit fluffy! The map!

BANANA. Melon is only a Corporal with little command responsibility. When his commanding officer gets him out of a tough scrape he bull shits the officer, making the commander think he's a congressional hero of honor, and a lot of times it works!

MELON. He wanted to leave you for the black vultures!

BANANA. He also does the reverse, ruining some officers because they make blunders!

MELON. He never read the map! Evidence!

BANANA. Corporal Melon has no equilibrium. He distorts the real conditions for his advantage. He's out of focus!

MELON. He's crazy! Insects, Cherry! Black vultures!

BANANA. That's your Melon, Cherry! . . . You went hunting in the city. You did everything together! What is everything, Corporal?

MELON. Get off, Banana!

BANANA. I know what you guys do! How big is Cherry?

MELON. That's enough!

BANANA. Eight inches? Uh? (*Pushes point of gun in* MELON's *face.*) This is big enough! Can you take all this?

MELON. Cut it!

BANANA. It's perfect for your big hot mouth! Suck!
Don't stop! Suck it! Suck cock! You cocksucker! Suck!
MELON. You faggot!
BANANA. Wha? Uhhh! Ehhhh!

(BANANA *grabs* MELON *and they fight struggling on
feet. They move to down center . . . Loud burst
of machine gun fire and flashing strobe light.*
BANANA *and* MELON *fall to floor.* MELON *is killed
by machine gun.*)

CHERRY. Corporal! Corporal! Lieutenant! Are you hit?
What happened? Answer me! Lieutenant!

(BANANA *crawls from dead* MELON *down stage
center to* CHERRY *up stage center and sits legs
and arms folded.*

Organist plays implacable background.)
Where's the Corporal?

BANANA. Over there, next to the bush.
CHERRY. What do you mean? What's he doing?
BANANA. He's dead.
CHERRY. *Dead?* . . . dead . . . You killed him, Lieu-
tenant!
BANANA. No. They did!
CHERRY. You killed him! Your lies killed him! The
Lieutenant was supposed to be infallible . . . the supreme
authority and the god damn know it all show off tops!
You're slipping! No. You fell, and can't get up! When the
Corporal confronted you with the map and the facts you
couldn't admit to them. Blundering has always been
outside your realm. Hasn't it? And so you thought you
could stop him from telling me the truth about our
position. You hit him. Didn't you realize that once he
started to peel you, that was it? You were finished because I always believed in the Corporal. He never
knocked a man unless he was absolutely, positively sure.
What did you want to do after I was shot? Keep running?
Leave me for the enemy! Black vultures? Insects? *You*
left the others to die! We left them behind! So, Lieutenant! What do you think? Uhh?
BANANA. They did!
CHERRY. Whaaat? . . . When are they coming to
finish us? Five hours? Now? Twenty minutes . . . afraid?
What's left for us to do? My leg's shot up and I'm high

on that stuff but I can think and it's more than you can
do! Yeah! Okay man. It's hopeless. So we'll make believe!
I'll take the first watch while you rest, then you'll relieve me and then I'll sleep. You understand?

BANANA. Yes, Private. Private First Class.

CHERRY. You'd better repeat what I said, I'm not
sure you understood me and it's important to me that
you did understand what I said because, *I want to dream*
tonight!

BANANA. You said you would take the first watch
and I'm supposed to rest and then I would relieve you
so that you could dream.

(*Organist stops playing.*)

CHERRY. Miraculous metal man! Sleep, Lieutenant.
You better do some dreaming! There's nothing else!

> (CHERRY *stands and marches slowly with limp to
> dead* MELON *down stage center.* CHERRY *props
> dead* MELON *up into sitting position, holding him
> from behind.* CHERRY *pathetically and sensuously
> kisses dead* MELON's *neck.* CHERRY *cries softly as he
> touches* MELON's *ears.*)

Hey Lieutenant! There's nobody to keep you company!
Lieutenant Banana! Who do you have? The insects? Say
something, Banana! What do you think? Uh? Come on!
Get out! What do you think? Uh? What the hell are
you waiting for? Are you awake, Banana?

BANANA. How can I sleep with you bull shittin'?

CHERRY. You know it all! Tell me everything!

> (FILM: *Film on screen up stage center shows close-
> up of fruit salad as girl slowly stirs . . .* BANANA,
> *in his modern New York apartment, fills book-
> shelf with books . . . Close-up of his lustrous long
> brunette haired girlfriend sitting in living room
> waiting for him.* BANANA, *wearing suit-shirt-tie, lifts
> plastic cover of hi-fi turntable and plays record . . .
> Shot of slightly irritable girlfriend, she's still wait-
> ing for him.* BANANA *mixes cocktails in glass pitcher
> and stirs thoroughly. He approaches irritable girl-
> friend and hands her drink.* BANANA *looks at her
> with marked inhibition . . . Close-up of salad girl
> stirring fruit salad . . . Close-up of smiling fruit
> salad girl.*)

BANANA moves to down stage center, joining CHERRY *and dead* MELON. CHERRY *leaves* MELON *alone.*)

BANANA. What do you want to know, Cherry?

CHERRY. Everything!

BANANA. We're cut off! You're skinned! I'm peeled! Melon's chopped up! We're all mixed and ready to eat! (*Stands looking over the heads of audience.*) Enemies run and hide! We seek them out and kill them. Then we run —hide and they search for us—kill us! Killing is for real men! It's no kid's game! So get your Private First Class ass over there and dream off! I'm still in command, move mister!

CHERRY. Yes sir.

(CHERRY *stands and marches to area up stage center and lies on floor. He sleeps and dreams.* BANANA *is down stage center.*)

BANANA (*yelling, screaming insanely*). Waaaaarrrr-rrr!!!!! (*Tormentedly.*) What for!? Power? Is glory! Glory is a feeling! A sensation, an emotion! War is destruction . . . annihilation . . . extinction . . . doom! *War eats men!* Shits death! Piss lies! Excuses become hungry from over-fatigue delusions! Vomiting contradictions follow the leader to confuse! Fungus, the insects, open stomachs! Commanding beliefs to disintegrate into Simon Says cuts! Pus oozes from wounds, thin walls of skin break away easy, soaked swatches of gauze STOP, fluids are escaping! Hide and go seek HATE! (*Quickly walks over to sleeping* CHERRY, *up stage center, and bends down looking at* CHERRY.) Hey Private! You asleep? Cherry?

CHERRY. Uhhh? Whaaa? Ummm? What's going on? Uhh? Who are you?

BANANA. It's Banana!

CHERRY. Uhhhmmm?

BANANA. I'm the Banana! Who am I? Uhh?

CHERRY. The Banana.

BANANA. And you're the Cherry! Who are you? Uhh? Say it!

CHERRY. The Cherry.

BANANA. The Banana likes the Cherry! Come on! Say it!

CHERRY. Get the hell out of here! Leave me alone!

BANANA. Listen boy! I'm not going to make believe! You're going to do this and I'm going to do that and we'll do everything! You're the Cherry! Now say it! The Banana likes the Cherry! Say it!

CHERRY. Banana likes the Cherry.

BANANA. Banana likes the Cherry like the Banana likes the Cherry. You know what I mean? Now say this! Banana gets the Cherry because the Cherry likes the Banana and he wants Cherry, RIGHT NOW!!!

(BANANA *seduces* CHERRY *and they have sex tenderly.*)

Banana says do this!

CHERRY. May I?

BANANA. Yes you may! Now do that!

CHERRY. May I, Banana?

BANANA. You certainly may! Everything. Everything! Banana says do this . . . Do that . . . Ahhhhhhhhhhh!

(FILM: *On film screen up center, we see shots and slow pans showing barren branches of trees against pure blue sky. Organist plays serious-romantic music.*

BANANA *and* CHERRY *continue having sex tenderly, moving in unison.*

Picturization of the above scene is as follows: Up stage center we see BANANA *and* CHERRY *having tender sex, and directly above them on motion picture screen, we see various barren branches of trees against blue sky. Organist plays serious-romantic music up stage right and dead* MELON *lies on floor, down stage left.*

BANANA *and* CHERRY *finish having sex and as they ashamedly move apart both are shot by loud burst of machine gun and flashing strobe light. They die sprawled across each other.*

The stage is blacked out and there's a moment of silence.

FILM: *Film begins with individual close-ups of* MELON, BANANA *and* CHERRY *at different stages of disrobing their civilian clothes worn in previous sequences . . . Close-ups of* MELON, BANANA *and* CHERRY *showing them separately putting on their brightly colored coverall stage uniforms and silver helmets . . . Individual close-ups of them standing at attention.*)

ACTORS ON TAPE (*calling, echoing each other's names getting louder, then softer . . . louder to extremely loud distorted blasts*). Banana? Cherry? Melon! Cherry? Banana! Melon! Cherry, Melon, Banana! Cherry MELON-BANANA!!!!

(*A short pause.*

FILM: *Black and white Army training film shows close-up of Sergeant-narrator . . . close-up of* MELON *eating slice of Melon . . . shot of soldiers loading recoilless rifle in black and white . . . soldiers landing on beach in bw . . . soldier working on large maps in office in bw . . .* CHERRY *eating cherries . . .* BANANA *eating banana . . .* MELON *eating slice of melon . . . soldiers firing recoilless rifle . . . loading rifle, firing rifle in bw. Quick cuts:* CHERRY, BANANA, *fruit salad girl smiling,* MELON, *Sergeant-narrator, salad girl,* CHERRY, BANANA, *salad girl smiling.*)

ON TAPE (*small bits of training film Sergeant's narration are asynchronous, running slightly behind picture*).

SERGEANT-NARRATOR. Each man has a job . . . thorough training . . . We try to give . . . studying of maps . . . (*Etc.*)

ACTORS ON TAPE (*building from soft to loud*). Kill! Kill! Kill! KILL! KILL! KILL, KILL! KILLKILLKILL!

(*Huge explosion sounds with flashing strobe light.*

FILM: *Film on screen up stage center shows flashing colors . . . Pretty girl bends over fruit salad bowl and slowly eats fruit salad with shiny big spoon. Orchestra plays perky light and frivolous theme. Pretty girl finishes eating and stands smiling at audience.*

Stage is completely blacked out.)

ACTORS ON TAPE (*sounds of footsteps in the bush*).

MELON. Lieutenant! Over here! There's a dead one here!

(*Running footsteps stop. Dead* MELON *is lit down stage left.*)

BANANA. Looks as though he never had a choice!

MELON. What was he doing out here all by himself?

BANANA. Who knows, Corporal?

CHERRY. I'm going to have a look around, for valubles! I want souvenirs!

BANANA. You anticipated my command, Private! Take the stars, they're valuable!

(*Footsteps in the bush are heard.*)

We can't hang around here too long, Corporal. The others will be at the ravine, waiting for us!

CHERRY. Over here, you guys! On the double!

(*Running footsteps in the bush are heard.*)

BANANA. What is it?

(*Dead and entangled* BANANA *and* CHERRY *are lit up stage center.*)

CHERRY. Man, look at these two! I'm going to puke!

BANANA. It's a sad sight. Remind me to demand an investigation when we get to the ravine!

MELON. Chopped down right in the act! Shit! Shit on the bastards who cut them down!

CHERRY. Kill 'em mother fuckers!

BANANA. Save it for later! Okay, MEN!!! Move out!

(FILM: *We see flashing colors on screen. Fruit salad girl stands before salad bowl and wipes her mouth delicately and correctly with a napkin. Orchestra plays carefree sweeping waltz and perky light theme. Full close-up of smiling salad girl. Orchestra stops playing. Organist, up stage right, plays postlude; heavy foreboding theme which then changes to very full discordant ominous chords . . . a small sequence of chimes is heard. House lights are slowly lit. Organist continues with slightly ecclesiastical soothing material. Actors slowly evolve from dead positions and assume standing position for bows. Organist finishes on flippant note. He turns out light, rises and exits carrying sheet music.*)

ISTANBOUL

Rochelle Owens

Playbill for Premiere Production

ISTANBUL
by Rochelle Owens

Presented at Judson Poets' Theatre
(Judson Memorial Church, New York City)

Directed by Lawrence Kornfeld

CAST IN ORDER OF APPEARANCE

ROBED MAN ....George Economou

LEO ....Jamil Zakkai

GODFRIGH ....Michael Elias

BALDWIN ....Henry Proach

ZOE ....Caroline Elias

MARY ....Ann Linden

ALICE ....Chrystal Field

GERTRUDE ....Joan Astley

ST. MARY OF EGYPT ....Florence Tarlow

Assistant director: John Hendricks
Set: Malcolm Spooner
Lighting technician: Stephen Lamb
Technical assistants: Susan Blowers, Janice Saunders, Simon Byun, Karl Herreshoff

---

ROCHELLE OWENS

"My poetry has been published in many literary magazines. My plays *The String Game* and *Istanboul* were produced by the Judson Poets' Theatre under the direction of Lawrence Kornfeld. The La Mama Troupe toured Europe with my play *Homo* last year; the La Mama Troupe is currently presenting *Futz* under the direction of Tom O'Horgan.

"*Futz* was presented at the Minnesota Theatre Company in their workshop program in October, 1966. *Futz* will be seen in Europe when the La Mama Troupe tours again. My most recent play, *Beclch*, was produced at The Theatre of the Living Arts in Philadelphia. Andre Gregory directed the production and excerpts from the play were shown on New York City's WNDT television [Channel 13]. *Futz* was published in *New American Plays*, Volume II, by Hill & Wang."

SCENE I

(In a tavern in 15th century Constantinople, two men from Normandy, GODFRIGH *and* BALDWIN, *watch* LEO *(a Byzantine) dance. Another Byzantine, a* ROBED MAN, *watches: his face reflects the mood of the exotic music. Two* BYZANTINE WOMEN *watch also.)*

GODFRIGH.   He could ram my wife in the arm-pit!

BALDWIN.   What?

GODFRIGH.   He could ram Alice, my wife, in the arm-pit!

BALDWIN.   What? What do you mean?

GODFRIGH.   I mean if Alice was near him—look how he moves—some part of him would ram into her!

BALDWIN.   Are you kidding?

GODFRIGH.   Just let the schismatic try though—just let him try—I'll cut off his balls!

BALDWIN.   O is that what rammed into her? He'd be a eunuch if you cut his balls off. It's no crime in Constantinople, the Patriarch's a eunuch.

GODFRIGH.   He is? But that's not Christian! That's not human!

BALDWIN.   A eunuch's just got scales where his cock should be.

GODFRIGH.   He does? How do you know he has scales?

BALDWIN.   Because I buggered one once.

(Both laugh.)

GODFRIGH.   I wonder if the Patriarch's been buggered, the Holy Father of the East.

BALDWIN.   Probably—he's Greek!

GODFRIGH *(points to the* ROBED MAN*)*.   Always that same look, that same look of of . . .

143

BALDWIN. Superiority.

GODFRIGH. That's right! A look of superiority—like he could make gold out of piss!

(*Women give annoyed looks at* GODFRIGH *and* BALDWIN.)

ZOE. Sirs, we are watching the young man dance!

MARY. Your voices are interfering with the music— it will disturb the dancer!

GODFRIGH. O we are very sorry, we are so very sorry. We are so new in fair Constantinople—we don't know just how to behave. (*Winks at* BALDWIN.) But tell us, is it right for women, obviously high-born women like yourselves, to watch a man dance?

BALDWIN. The ladies back home, in our land, are kept in seclusion—very often with the belt and buckle on them.

ZOE. Belt and buckle?

MARY. Belt and buckle—a chastity belt?

GODFRIGH. That's right—so we KNOW THAT THEY MIGHT BE FAITHFUL TO US THEIR CHRISTIAN HUSBANDS!

ZOE. BUT THAT IS BARBARIC!

BALDWIN. SO IS CUTTING OFF A MAN'S BALLS!

MARY. Ahhhh—but that is a different thing, hereditary titles are kept in families that way.

ZOE. And did you know that some of our best military men are eunuchs? It's a myth that a eunuch has to get LETHARGIC AND FAT! And they are VERY PATRIOTIC!

MARY. Constantinople's eunuchs are indeed VERY PATRIOTIC! Indeed THE WHOLE EMPIRE'S EUNUCHS!

BALDWIN. Tell me fair lady, are all the men in Constantinople eunuchs?

MARY. O no sir, not ALL the men—why just look at the dancer—he's as whole as any man might be!

ZOE. He moves so charmingly—he makes me feel like I have drunk an elixir! O WE MUST STOP ALL THIS TALK AND WATCH THE DANCER!

MARY. His beauty and vigor make me feel so happy!

GODFRIGH. Mightn't I be able to make you feel happy? We could have some kebobs and hashish, then you could teach me how to dance and then . . .

MARY. Then what, sir?

GODFRIGH. Then we could fuck.

MARY. Fuck? What—what does that mean? I never heard the word fuck. I suppose it is a Latin word—it's certainly not Greek!

BALDWIN (*laughing with* GODFRIGH). Let me teach you a song, ladies—a song FROM THE WEST!

> I love coffee
> I love tea
> I love the java
> and the java loves me
> coffee and tea
> the java and me
> a fucka fucka fucka
> fucka you!

(*The* WOMEN *try to sing,* BALDWIN *enunciating words seriously,* GODFRIGH *laughing,* ROBED MAN *has cynical look on face.* LEO *stops dancing, looks furiously at them.*)

LEO. YOU FRUSTRATED WILD IDIOTS! HOW DARE YOU—HOW DARE YOU TEACH THAT WORD TO THESE INNOCENT WOMEN!

BALDWIN (*laughs*). Can't you take a good joke?

GODFRIGH. By the holy Father the true representative of Christ—we were having a little fun—just a little fun!

LEO. Is that what is called fun in the BARBARIC WEST? Teaching women LEWD COLLOQUIAL WORDS—IGNORANT NUTS! BOORS!

GODFRIGH (*to* BALDWIN). Should I beat him? Should I teach this heretic-pig how to bow?

BALDWIN. CHRIST'S MOTHER! LET'S JUST TAKE THESE TWO LITTLE LADIES!

ZOE. TAKE THESE TWO LITTLE LADIES! O NO YOU WON'T!

MARY. You ARE BOORS! LEO IS RIGHT! YOU ARE BOORS BOORS BOORS!

ZOE. Rough AND STUPID—BOORS!

MARY. AND ANIMALISTIC—BOORS!

LEO. See—WE KNOW WHO YOU ARE! We Byzan-

tines are sure of WHO AND WHAT YOU ARE! AND
WE KNOW WHO WE ARE!

BALDWIN. We came here just to talk to some women
and listen to some music—BUT YOU ARE MAKING
ME ITCH NOW!

GODFRIGH. Let's teach THE EAST, THIS IMPERIAL
CIVILIZATION—HOW TO HAIL THE POPE! BUT
FIRST I WANT TO SOFTEN THE BONES OF HIS
FACE!

(*He strikes* LEO *who deftly darts about blocking the
blows, the* WOMEN *rush in front of* LEO.)

MARY. DON'T YOU TOUCH HIM! LEAVE HIM
ALONE! KEEP AWAY FROM HIM!

ZOE. We'll climb in your hair if you hurt Leo!

(*The* WOMEN *embrace* LEO; ZOE *cries*.)

LEO (*to* GODFRIGH *and* BALDWIN). Your kind likes to
see women cry!

ZOE. Just me, Leo. I am the one who cries—Mary
does not.

MARY. I do not cry because I am secure in your love,
Leo. (*She grabs him.*)

ZOE. Do you not love me, Leo?

LEO. Mary and I are old friends, Zoe.

(GODFRIGH *and* BALDWIN *watch in surprise.*)

ZOE. But I know—I want you to dance with me
though.

LEO. Mary and I are old friends. We want to talk.

(ZOE *clutches at* LEO. MARY *is clutching too.* LEO *has
his arms around both but he yields to* MARY *more,*
ZOE *presses against him.*)

ZOE. I think you must think I'm a . . .

LEO. Why do you do this?

ZOE. I think I'm going to cry again. Do you want
me to cry?

LEO. No.

MARY (*to* ZOE, *surprised at her emotion*). You are
romantic!

ZOE. I can't help it. I can't HELP THE WAY I
FEEL ABOUT LEO.

LEO. I know I'm sexy.

ZOE. O IT'S NOT JUST SEX—a lot of men are sexy.

LEO. They are?

ZOE. But you have a sweetness . . .

MARY (*takes off shoes*). I WANT TO DANCE, LEO. I WANT YOU TO TEACH ME THE NEW SYRIAN DANCE!

(LEO *and* MARY *start to dance.*)

ZOE (*takes off shoes*). I HAVE GOT MY SHOES OFF TOO, LEO. I WANT TO DANCE TOO!

MARY. STOP YOUR RANTING, ZOE! Leo and I are GREAT TOGETHER! Just go away.

ZOE. YOU FAT CAT—I WON'T GO AWAY!

LEO. I don't like insults, Zoe—you've insulted Mary!

ZOE. I don't care—I DON'T CARE.

(*She screams and dives into* MARY, *the two fight.* LEO *goes to separate them.*)

LEO. You are acting like the FRANKISH WOMEN! LIKE CATS IN HEAT! STOP FIGHTING STOP FIGHTING STOP FIGHTING!

(*He cries, the* WOMEN *stop fighting, tenderly look at him, they put their arms around him and each other. The* ROBED MAN *watches them.*)

SCENE II

(*In the bedroom of* GODFRIGH's *wife* ALICE. *She is with her friend* GERTRUDE.)

ALICE. Sometimes when Godfrigh was so light-headed from the mead—he'd tell his filthy jokes—and then he'd begin to stare—AT MY ARM-PITS!

GERTRUDE. Maybe he had a thing with arm-pits. Did he tell jokes about arm-pits?

ALICE. Yes! All of them, evil jokes!

GERTRUDE. Tell one!

ALICE. You mean one of his arm-pit jokes?

GERTRUDE. Yes!

ALICE. O it's stupid! Well—but it's so stupid! I could never understand WHY it was so funny to him. One time there was a woman who was all lop-sided. Her ears were set wrongly and her nose was where her mouth should be and vice-versa. So this woman went to bed with a man and when she undressed the man laughed and she got angry and she said if you don't stop your laughing I'll pee on you whereupon she lifted up her arm and peed on him.

GERTRUDE. BIZARRE!

ALICE. Yes, I think so too! You know he never wanted me to SHAVE MY LEGS! I am not a hairy woman . . .

GERTRUDE. I am not either.

ALICE. But the little I do have, he said that I should keep—I DIDN'T LIKE THAT! I LIKE MY LEGS TO BE SMOOTH!

GERTRUDE. Me too.

ALICE. He'd tell me about the Byzantine women and how HAIRY SOME OF THEM WERE—and how it made him HOT to think about them.

GERTRUDE. UGH!

ALICE (*bitterly*). He never appreciated my smoothness.

GERTRUDE. I hear some of these Eastern women rub chalk on their bellies to make whiter!

ALICE. I am not at all surprised, they DO and KNOW a lot of ways to please a man—and then after FORTY YEARS of fucking and sucking—THEY JOIN A CONVENT—BECOME NUNS!

GERTRUDE. They are a superstitious bunch.

ALICE. And their murky intrigues! Their rotten double-dealings—the Empress Irene putting out the EYES OF HER OWN SON!

GERTRUDE. AND THEY LOOK DOWN ON US! WE ARE CALLED THE BARBARIANS!

ALICE. I hate the guts of Constantinople! I knew a Bulgar man once—and he said that Constantinople AND THE WHOLE EMPIRE WOULD BE DESTROYED BY GOD!

GERTRUDE. Like Sodom and Gomorrah!

ALICE. Now SOME of the Byzantine men are quite nice though—they have a sweetness.

GERTRUDE. I guess there's always some good among the bad—IT'S THE WOMEN I HATE!

ALICE. The men have a feeling for spirituality I think. They are different from our men of the West.

GERTRUDE. And they have such beautiful eyes and such charming manners—AND HOW THEY DANCE! AND I'VE NEVER SEEN ONE DRUNK!

ALICE. Yes—the men are quite nice—one of them once said to me, his name is Leo, "Alice, you chew food like a woman, your jaw moves so beautifully as you chew." We were having dinner of roasted lamb, when he said that. "Alice, I am deathless when I am near you," he said.

GERTRUDE. Lovely, lovely—that's something Godfrigh would never think of saying—that's POETRY!

ALICE. His face is so beautiful: Leo's. Do you know he modelled for one of the great Armenian artists? He was St. George with a golden halo around his head—his sweetness.

GERTRUDE. I like a man to be sweet.

ALICE. Well, Leo is very sweet—he's ninety-nine and three quarters per-cent why I am able to go on living in Constantinople. If it weren't for him I'd have made Godfrigh send me home a long time ago. Do you know that when I first met Leo—during one of our little talks—he looked at me and said that he imagined my belly as being as smooth as the statue of Aphrodite—Leo never said it—but I think he doesn't like HAIRY WOMEN—the opposite of Godfrigh who thinks the hairier the better!

GERTRUDE. Perverted perverted!

ALICE. One time Godfrigh made me wear a pair of little SLAVIC FUR PANTS!

GERTRUDE. To keep you warm?

ALICE. TO GET HIM HOT!

GERTRUDE. Weird weird!

ALICE. Hair, fur, fuzzy things, AND HE BRAGGED ABOUT IT—HE SAID A MAN SHOULD BE UNIQUE!

GERTRUDE. A pair of little Slavic fur pants—and that made him hot—when YOU wore it?

ALICE. O, yes.

GERTRUDE. No wonder he won't leave Byzantium—all these HAIRY WOMEN AROUND!

ALICE. That's right plus the fact he thinks he might be able to get rich here—then he'll go to Jerusalem on a pilgrimage—and get his SINS FORGIVEN!

GERTRUDE. O no—not that again! I've heard that story a hundred times—they all say it—all the knights—that they'll fight the Saracens for the sake of the Holy City—but they never go!

ALICE.   Why should they? Here is where the fun and riches are! Hypocrites WHAT HYPOCRITES! Jerusalem is always a pretext for getting to Constantinople!

GERTRUDE.   Nothing like a holy reason for a sinning need. By the way where is Godfrigh?

ALICE.   O he went with Baldwin and some Armenian to one of the provinces—about buying some shrine. A SHRINE! Can you imagine!

GERTRUDE.   A shrine? You mean, a holy place?

ALICE.   Exactly! One of the Eastern provinces—I forget which one, is having a commercial boom, thousands of merchants from all over the world are pouring in. Godfrigh thinks buying a shrine and some land would be a way—a good way—TO GET RICH—you know—selling relics!

GERTRUDE.   Ohh—well these Easterners are very religious.

ALICE.   Religious HAH! FANATICAL! And they LOVE relics—give them a cruddy toe, say it came from the corpse of St. Christodulus or somebody—and they'll eat it up with devotion! Any dribbling beggar might be a SAINT—as long as he's FILTHY ENOUGH!

GERTRUDE.   Disgusting!

ALICE.   These schismatics are no better than Moslems or Jews! Gertrude, I really must attend to some business now . . .

GERTRUDE.   Of course—I have visited much too long already. Adieu.

ALICE.   Adieu.

    (GERTRUDE *exits,* ALICE *takes off her dress, puts on a filmy thing, primps.* LEO *enters.*)

O my sweet prince of the East! I am so glad thou hast come to me!

LEO.   I'm glad that you asked me, Alice. (*He kisses her.*)

ALICE.   I love to feel your shoulders, your arms—and thou hast such beautiful eyes—as beautiful as a Turk's!

LEO.   Humm yes—it's the make-up—I haven't had a chance to take it off—just left the tavern a little while ago.

ALICE.   How many women were following thee while thou were walking to me—three, four?

LEO. No women followed me, Alice.

ALICE. O I've heard about thee—how thou hast all the women and the virgins burning for thee!

LEO. Rumors! Don't talk with thees and thous.

ALICE. Why?

(*They kiss.*)

LEO. Because they sound silly.

ALICE. Don't hurt my feelings, Leo. I want to use them—it seems right with you—O when I see you I cannot help but KNOW why women love you! I cannot help but want to say the words from "The Song of Songs."

> O to feel the kiss of thy lips
> for thy love is better than wine!
> Sweet to the smell are thine ointments
> thy name is as perfume poured forth
> No wonder the maidens adore thee!
> O take me away! Let us hasten
> that my King may bring me to his room.
> There in gladness and joy of thee
> we will extol thy love more than wine.
> How right they are to adore thee!

(*They kiss, drink wine.*)

LEO. You know, Alice—sometimes women only want the outside of a man—like his bone structure . . .

ALICE (*sexy*). . . . and his lips and his hips and his long . . . eyelashes.

LEO. I don't have a cloven hoof!

ALICE. What do you mean?

LEO. I am not just full of lust—and you do have a husband.

ALICE. So?

LEO. Thou shalt not covet another man's wife.

ALICE. O sweetheart I am coveting thee!

(*They kiss,* GERTRUDE'*s voice is heard offstage.*)

GERTRUDE. ALICE, IT'S GERTRUDE—I'VE FORGOTTEN MY PARASOL!

ALICE (*angry*). O—well—why did you forget it! O NEVER MIND—COME IN!

(GERTRUDE *enters, sees* LEO *and grins.*)

Leo, this is Gertrude.

LEO. Hello, Gertrude.

GERTRUDE. Hello, Leo—WHY YOU LOOK LIKE— why you look like St. George!

(ALICE *frowns.*)

LEO. I am not half as holy. (*He smiles.*)

GERTRUDE. O I should hope not—and he was probably a eunuch. (*She winks.*)

LEO. And I am not.

GERTRUDE. O I should hope not.

(ALICE *gets parasol, hands it to* GERTRUDE.)

ALICE. Well—here's your parasol, Gertrude—take it and leave!

GERTRUDE. O I want to talk with you and Leo a little while—and I'm quite tired—I had to walk all the way home before I realized I was lacking something . . . my parasol. (*Gives* LEO *sexy look.*)

LEO. You are not acting friendly, Alice. Gertrude should stay and rest awhile. She looks so pale.

GERTRUDE. I am so fair too . . . O BUT I AM FAINT TOO! (*She goes to bed and lies down.*) O Alice, I would love a little wine—this heat of Constantinople— please, a little wine.

ALICE. No wine for Gertrude.

LEO. What? Of course wine for Gertrude! (*He pours wine and hands it to* GERTRUDE.)

GERTRUDE. Cranky, cranky Alice—poor Alice wears such tight girdles—they give her headaches.

ALICE. You didn't have to say that!

GERTRUDE. I wanted Leo to know the reason for your rudeness, Alice. When we know a reason for a thing— then we can understand it.

LEO. Is it the tight girdles that give you headaches, Alice?

ALICE. No! It's not the tight girdles! AND GOD- DAMN IT I WEAR ONLY ONE AT A TIME!—AND NOW I'M NOT WEARING ANY!

LEO. ALICE—what has gotten into you!

GERTRUDE. Headaches—she gets headaches—they make her irrational!

ALICE. IRRATIONAL! YOU ITCHING BITCH! GET OUT OF MY BED!

(*She lunges at* GERTRUDE, *they fight on bed, fall off fighting,* LEO *tries to stop them.*)

LEO. STOP IT MAD-WOMEN! HASHISH-MAD FEMALES! CRAZY-WOMEN! STOP IT! STOP IT!

ALICE. GET OUT GERTRUDE! GET OUT! GET OUT! GET OUT!

GERTRUDE. DON'T THINK I WON'T! YOU'RE SICK!
(*She gets up, tidies herself and leaves.*)

ALICE (*hysterical*). Malicious obscene cat! OHHHH-HHHH!

LEO. All right, pomegranate—I saw through her . . .

ALICE. You did? Then why did you encourage her?

LEO. O I didn't realize . . .

ALICE. Didn't realize? What?

LEO. Well—women sometimes baffle me—I try to be helpful and then something always happens.

ALICE (*crying*). O my nose—she hurt my nose!

LEO. O poor little pomegranate . . .

ALICE. My nose—my nose—it hurts!

LEO. Yes, sweet one—your nose hurts—but it will feel better—Leo will kiss it.

ALICE. O kiss my nose, Leo—make it better.

(*He kisses nose.*)

O I want some hashish mmmmm hashish.

LEO. Leo will give his little pomegranate some hashish —in just a minute.

ALICE. IN JUST A MINUTE! THE BLESSED VIR-GIN! MY HUSBAND MIGHT BE BACK IN JUST A MINUTE!

LEO. HE MIGHT? O THE BLESSED VIRGIN! (*He runs to door.*)

ALICE (*laughing*). No, no Leo—I am pretending! It's exciting to me—to feel that at any minute—my husband might walk in!—AND FIND US FUCKING, or just about to!

LEO. Pretending—you mean he won't be back any minute?

ALICE (*laughing*). NO, LEO, NO—HE'S FAR AWAY!

LEO. Funny—so funny.

ALICE. O I am not just laughing because of the fun-niness—I am laughing because of the EXCITEMENT! THE EXCITEMENT! THE EXCITEMENT!

LEO (*tired*). How many times are you going to repeat the word EXCITEMENT!

ALICE. O LEO THINK OF IT! O I'VE THOUGHT
OF IT SO MANY TIMES! YOU AND I IN THE ACT!
—AND THEN SOMEBODY WALKS IN!

LEO. First you talk about your husband walking in—
and now it's SOMEBODY WALKING IN—SOON IT'LL
BE ANYBODY WALKING IN!

ALICE. THAT'S RIGHT, LEO! ANYBODY WALK-
ING IN WHILE WE WERE IN THE ACT! ANYBODY
WOULD BE VERY EXCITING—FOR ME AND FOR
YOU!

LEO. Are you kidding! I'm not nuts! You know—I really
think you're nuts! I think Gertrude must have hurt your
brains and not just your nose!

ALICE (*laughing*). Gertrude—Now if she had come
while we were making love—then I wouldn't have gotten
mad—ANYBODY WILL DO—ANYBODY WILL GIVE
ME THIS EXCITEMENT—AS LONG AS THEY HAVE
EYES TO WATCH US!

LEO. Watch us?

ALICE. Watch us fucking!—O don't be so innocent—
people liking to be watched is no *new* thing—the old
Romans watched each other like crazy!

LEO. Alice, you are crazy! I don't understand—I really
don't understand you—AND TO BE VERY TRUTHFUL
—I WISH I WERE IN EGYPT NOW—FAR AWAY
FROM YOU!

ALICE (*grabs him*). O DON'T SAY THAT! DON'T
SAY THAT! DON'T EVER SAY YOU WANT TO BE
FAR AWAY FROM ME!

LEO. The things you are saying—I feel as though ants
are CRAWLING ON ME! PEOPLE WATCHING US
WHILE WE'RE FUCKING, GERTRUDE, SOMEBODY,
ANYBODY, OLD ROMANS . . .

ALICE. All right Leo—FORGET IT! JUST SOME
SILLY IDEAS—reading Ovid—he talks about things like
that . . .

LEO. NO HE DOESN'T!—Ovid never talks ABOUT
BEING WATCHED WHILE LOVE-MAKING—AND
YOU KNOW IT! YOU JUST MADE THAT UP!

ALICE. All right! I MADE IT UP!

LEO. Now why, Alice—why do you say things like that?

ALICE. Ooo I don't know. Darling, I'm tired—Don't be so critical—don't harp at me—just be sweet and hold me. (*Embraces him.*) Leo, now sing to me—sing to me the newest chant from Syria.

(*He sings.*)

Now let's make love—without being watched.

(*They kiss.*)

Leo, have you ever seen Slavic fur pants?

SCENE III

(*In a dismal ugly tavern.* GODFRIGH *and* BALDWIN *are drinking wine; the* ROBED MAN *is there; soft music plays.*)

BALDWIN. If we don't get a disease by the time we leave Constantinople—I'll think it's a miracle!

GODFRIGH. Why?

BALDWIN. This place! This tavern is one of the filthiest in Constantinople! Why do we come here? Why are you always making me sit here with you?

GODFRIGH. Don't put everything on me—you want to get riches too—you want to make an eventual pilgrimage to the Holy City too!

BALDWIN. What has that to do with this disgusting place?

GODFRIGH. I'll tell you—this place has a lot to do with what we want—namely riches!

BALDWIN. O yes—and I'm Jesus son of Mary!

GODFRIGH. Do you agree that the Armenians are the best businessmen?

BALDWIN. Well, what does that have to . . .

GODFRIGH. Just answer my question—are the Armenians good businessmen?

BALDWIN. Yes, and so are the Greeks!

GODFRIGH. Well, Beshar the Armenian—you met him the other day—said that if we really want to attract people to the shrine—we should have a REAL LIVE SAINT!

BALDWIN. A what?

GODFRIGH. A LIVING SAINT!

BALDWIN. Yes—AHAH! A SAINT!

GODFRIGH. I am very serious. A saint to attract people to my shrine.

BALDWIN. Our shrine! My money's in this venture too.

GODFRIGH. That's better. Our shrine. The Easterners as you are well aware of by now, are wild about holiness, they love convents, monasteries, nuns, priests, ascetics AND SAINTS!

BALDWIN. Where are we going to find a saint?

GODFRIGH. In this place—this filthy place. Her name is St. Mary of Egypt—Beshar said she comes here sometimes, begging alms. We are waiting for her.

BALDWIN. We are?

GODFRIGH. Yes—but she must not know that we want to exploit her for commercial gain—otherwise she will never agree to come with us—SHE MUST NOT FIND OUT THAT SHE HERSELF WILL BE THE DRAW OF PEOPLE'S MONEY—she must think that the shrine is her SANCTUARY and not a place of business—our business. We'll have lots of things lying around—bits of the true cross, pieces of cloth from the garments of Jesus and his apostles—umm fingers, toes, hunks of hair—Mary will go around touching all these things—and people will BUY ANYTHING that she happens to touch! Think of all the relics we could sell—that St. Mary of Egypt has touched!

(ST. MARY OF EGYPT *enters, dirty, dressed in a hair-shirt, arms and legs hairy. She swings a bell.*)

BALDWIN (*whispers surprise*). Holy Mother!

GODFRIGH. Son of Mary!

ST. MARY (*chanting*).

> Saracens never touched me—I hid
> Saracens never touched me—I hid
> Saracens never sucked at these teats
> —I hid from them
> Unbelievers never touched me
> Unbelievers never touched me
> Unbelievers never sucked at these
> teats—I hid from them
> Virgin I am—virtuous I am

Holy Holy I am give money to St.
Mary of Egypt the pure one
She who will get you in heaven
with a prayer! She who will ask
Christ Pantocrator to smile on you!
Christ Pantocrator who never smiles
will smile on you—because of St.
Mary of Egypt!
Earthquakes swallowed up the Saracens
after they looked upon Mary's white
body—St. Mary's still a virgin
so give her some money.

(*She goes to table,* ROBED MAN *gives her a coin,
she approaches* GODFRIGH *and* BALDWIN.)

BALDWIN.   Here, pure mother. (*Gives coin.*)

GODFRIGH.   Pray for us, mother. (*Gives coin.*) Share
some wine with us, little mother.

BALDWIN.   Share our table with us—we who will go to
the Holy City to fight the Saracen-dogs!

ST. MARY.   You will go to the blessed city and on the
first day you will kill 600 Saracens! On the second day
700 Persians! On the third day 400 Turks! On the fourth
day 300 monophysites! And on the fifth, sixth and seventh
days YOU WILL KILL ALL THE MOSLEMS AND
JEWS! (*Gives long gasping laughter.*)

BALDWIN.   JERUSALEM FOR CHRISTIANS!

GODFRIGH.   JERUSALEM FOR CHRIST'S FOLLOW-
ERS!

ST. MARY (*breathes heavy*).
I'll sit down with you now,
eat some bread, drink some wine,
Christ's blood is wine you know,
his fair flesh whiter than bread you know,
his toe clutches the heart of the world,
the ends of his hair tickle the face of God,
wine, wine, the first drink I've had this
morning is this sip of wine,
bread, bread, the first bite I've had this
morning is this bread. (*Smiling, squinting.*)
You are two men from the north, your eyes
are light like Christ's eyes are light.

BALDWIN. From Normandy, little mother.

GODFRIGH. We have come all the way from Normandy.

ST. MARY. With your wives? Have you brought your wives? Constantinople's good for a wife, so many churches, good for a wife to be in the church, Constantinople's full of churches, wives should be in the churches.

GODFRIGH. Little Mother, my wife is with me—and she is always in Church!

ST. MARY. Is she an Eastern Christian?

GODFRIGH. No—for we are Western Christians, little mother. We heed the Pope.

ST. MARY. You're Christians all the same, West East Pope no hope, who will judge the separation between East and West? Certainly God will but we cannot with our human tongues say that we will judge whether the East is right or the West, I myself am a Greek though my grandfather was a Hittite, I follow the wisdom of the Greeks, I seek no sign like the Jews, ever since Christ saved me I wait to hear it from him, what the truth is, he tells me every night in my dreams, in my coffee cups, one time I turned my coffee cup over and I saw the image of God, he was in the form of a Bear, but I knew it was God because there in the middle of the bear's forehead, was the cross! A cross burning in the head of a bear!

GODFRIGH. A cross in the head of a bear!

ST. MARY. Yes, in the head of a bear, and I knew what it meant, a bear sways when he walks, his feet press hard the earth's floor, he is brown like the earth, he smells like the earth, and so I knew that the bear symbolized the world, and the cross symbolized God and the world and God were one! And then when I understood in my heart all these things, A GREAT WIND CAME OUT FROM BEHIND ME, AND I KNEW THAT A SARACEN HAD PUT A DEVIL IN ME, BUT AFTER KNOWING WHAT THE CROSS BURNING IN THE HEAD OF A BEAR MEANT—I HAD BEEN FORGIVEN BY GOD—AND THE DEVIL WENT OUT OF ME IN THE FORM OF WIND!

GODFRIGH. SARACENS! WE ARE IMPATIENT TO GET TO JERUSALEM! TO RID THE HOLY CITY OF THE HEATHENS!

BALDWIN. How I must get to Jerusalem—to walk where the Son of God walked—TO KILL HIS KILLERS!

ST. MARY. His killers, the Jews, they had the chance to know him but they knew him not, they had the chance to kiss him but they kissed him not, but Judas kissed him with betrayal, kissed God's son with his evil lips, beware of red-haired men: they are the SONS OF JUDAS! I saw a red-haired Saracen on an Aegean Island where I hid, I became very afraid because I knew he would try to kiss me if he found me, THE KISS OF BETRAYAL! But he never found me! Nor did the other Saracens find me because I hid from them, Saracens never touched me, never touched St. Mary of Egypt's sweet body.

GODFRIGH. Little mother, you hid on an Aegean Island, from the Saracens?

ST. MARY. Pirates, Saracen pirates, but I escaped from them, God made one of the Aegean Islands come up under me in the middle of the sea, there I was, the only one on the island, the Angel Gabriel brought me some rice and fish in a silver bowl, the rice lasted six years short of six months, the fish lasted seven years, God had provided for me until the Byzantines found me, naked I lived on the island, naked I was when they found me, covered with hair and dirt, my nails long as a dragon's, my teeth black like tar, but my BREATH WAS AS SWEET AS A BABY'S!

GODFRIGH. Did you say you were covered with hair?

ST. MARY. Ahhh yes—this hair-shirt that I wear was made from the hair of my own body.

GODFRIGH. It is?

ST. MARY. Ahhh yes—and you should have seen my legs . . .

GODFRIGH. I should have?

ST. MARY. They thought I was an animal so hairy was I—I looked as though I was covered with black fur!

GODFRIGH. Black fur! I would not have thought you were an animal—I would have known you were a woman.

ST. MARY. I DID LOOK LIKE AN ANIMAL, AN ANIMAL WITH DARK HAIR, BREASTS, ARMS, LEGS, BELLY, COVERED WITH HAIR, DIRTY HAIR!

GODFRIGH. You never washed?

ST. MARY. NEVER—IT WAS MY CHOICE! MORTI-FICATION FOR THE SON OF GOD! I never washed nor cut my hair, there were sharp stones I could have cut my hair with, but I chose not to for HIS SAKE! FOR THE SAKE OF THE SON OF GOD!

GODFRIGH (*excited*). Do you know, St. Mary—I love hairy women!

BALDWIN (*nervous*). O yes—hairy women are fine—but, but Godfrigh, I think the little mother should know of the holy place. The shrine!

GODFRIGH. O, yes, the shrine. Because we love the Lord and our Christian faith, the Lord has chosen us to do his work, St. Mary of Egypt. And so he has made a way for us to serve him. He led us to sanctified ground where a miracle happened in the tenth century. A cruel Turk, a pagan, turned Christian, because of the love of a woman, a Christian woman who became a saint so much like you, pure mother. We have built a shrine on that holy ground. But, alas, it needs the blessed feet of a child of Christ to walk upon it, the holy ground. It needs the feet of St. Mary of Egypt! It needs the feet of St. Mary of Egypt to press into its sacred earth!

ST. MARY. The feet of me—ahhh, yes—and I have got the right feet (*Shows feet.*)—these feet. THESE FEET FLED FROM SARACENS! I RAN ON THEM FROM UNBELIEVERS!

BALDWIN. Come with us to the shrine God has shown to us, FOR YOU! MAKE THE HOLY GROUND IT RESTS ON HOLIER!

GODFRIGH (*to* ST. MARY). With your feet . . . (*Musing*). You have big legs . . .

ST. MARY. The biggest in the East! God gave me big legs so that I might flee from Saracens!

BALDWIN (*nervous*). Yes, the Saracens! But now CHRISTIANS are asking you to go the way of THE LORD . . .

ST. MARY. I always go THE LORD'S WAY!

BALDWIN. Yes—but to the shrine! The Lord has shown us the shrine—FOR YOU, PURE MOTHER!

ST. MARY. I like Constantinople—I won't leave—last night I had a dream—God came to me in the form of a giant oak tree and the leaves whispered (*Whispers.*) St.

Mary of Egypt must never leave Constantinople, if St. Mary goes from the city—the city will be destroyed by Saracens! I cannot go—I cannot leave Constantinople—I MUST STAY TO SAVE THE CITY! I have friends here, anyhow.

BALDWIN (*to* GODFRIGH). Well?

GODFRIGH. What do we know of heavenly things—we are shown the Lord's Way, and so is St. Mary of Egypt. WHO ARE WE COMPARED TO ST. MARY! . . . (*Softly.*) Are they as big up as they are around the calf?

ST. MARY. What?

GODFRIGH. Your legs.

BALDWIN (*angry*). Son of his mother—Godfrigh!

GODFRIGH. Go away, Baldwin! I want to talk alone with St. Mary.

BALDWIN (*disgusted*). All right! But remember—my money! (*He leaves.*)

GODFRIGH. Are they as big up as they are around the calf?

ST. MARY. Bigger—much bigger—AND SALTY!

GODFRIGH. Salty?

ST. MARY. Salt is a purifier! I rub it into the hair.

GODFRIGH. Of your legs? You rub salt into the hair of your legs?

ST. MARY. I SAID WHAT I SAID! The situation is this—had the manna been salty, the Israelites would have died of thirst in the desert! But the Lord made the manna SWEET—and so I commemorate the event by rubbing my body with salt—because my flesh is SWEET—as is the flesh of all God's saints! His living saints!

GODFRIGH. I don't understand . . .

ST. MARY. IT IS NOT FOR YOU TO UNDERSTAND GOD'S WAYS! MYSTERIOUS—HIS WAYS ARE MYSTERIOUS!

GODFRIGH. You have salt all over you now? Rubbed into the hair?

ST. MARY. AGAIN I SAY TO YOU I SAID WHAT I SAID!

GODFRIGH. Could I see it, sweet mother?

(*Extends her arm, he looks, rubs finger on it, tastes.*) (*Helplessly.*) Salty . . . Could I touch your big legs?

ST. MARY.   Saracens never touched me—I hid Saracens
never . . .

GODFRIGH.   But I'm a Christian! I'M A CHRISTIAN!
A CHRISTIAN!

(*He falls grovelling before her, his hands go up her
dress, lights go out except for soft purple light on
face of* ROBED MAN, *his expression is very cynical,
music plays loud, incense-smell.*)

SCENE IV

(*The tavern of the first scene,* MARY *and* ZOE *are
drinking wine. The* ROBED MAN *is there.*)

MARY.   I loved Thessaly. Leo loved Thessaly—we
fished naked on the hot days, after the fishing we would
swim—what fun! O, he loved me—but that was a long
time ago. I must be realistic!

ZOE.   Do you think that Leo still loves you?

MARY.   Of course! I know Leo—do you know he used
to cry whenever I left him?

ZOE.   Left him?

MARY.   O, well—other fish, you know. Other fish—and
I swam with them. Leo's only a tavern dancer—and I
want more than JUST a tavern dancer. I must be realistic!

ZOE.   Yes—you said that.

MARY.   Leo is a child!

ZOE.   O, but he's so beautiful!

MARY.   Mmmmmmyes—he LOVES my body—he always
went CRAZY over my ass, my breasts . . .

ZOE.   Agh! YOU ARE VILE!

MARY.   O, GO AWAY! WHAT ARE YOU HERE FOR!
I'M THE ONE WHO'S GOING TO BE WITH LEO!

ZOE.   I CAN SIT HERE TOO! THIS TAVERN IS
FOR EVERYONE!

MARY.   ANYONE—EVEN FOR BITCHES LIKE YOU!

ZOE.   YOU'RE THE BITCH, MARY!

MARY.   O, shut up! (*Changes her seat.*)

ZOE (*calling to her*).   YOU MUST HAVE LOOKED
LIKE A FAT COW—Hah, swimming naked!

MARY.   IF YOU DON'T SHUT UP—I'M GOING TO
TEAR . . .

(LEO *enters.*)

LEO. TEAR WHAT—WHAT ARE YOU GOING TO TEAR, MARY!

MARY. O, it's Zoe—she's always trying to hurt my feelings! Leo, tell her to go away from us!

LEO. Mary, I just work here—I can't tell Zoe to go, just as I can't tell you to go . . .

ZOE (*to* MARY). AHAH!

MARY (*gets up*). Well—ALL RIGHT! GOODBYE!
 (*As she is almost out the door,* GODFRIGH *rushes in, pushes her back in, he's drunk.*)

GODFRIGH. I've got a hairy woman! YAOW! I've found one—Come here, hairy woman!

MARY (*laughing*). O sir, you are gay! O, I remember you—where is your friend?
 (GODFRIGH *grabs her.*)
O sir, you ARE gay!

GODFRIGH. Gay, gay—I'm going to kiss you! (*He kisses.*)

LEO. LET GO OF THE WOMAN, FRANK!

GODFRIGH. Aaaaaaaaaaaahh I remember you—you're the woman protector—a hairy-woman-protector! (*He's hugging* MARY.) HAIRY WOMAN, KISS ME BACK!

MARY (*she kisses*). With all my heart!

LEO. DO YOU WANT TO BE MAN-HANDLED, MARY? BY THAT!

MARY (*does bump and grind into* GODFRIGH). WHAT'S WRONG WITH THAT!

GODFRIGH. Hairy woman you make me happy!

LEO (*runs to* MARY, *pushes her away from* GODFRIGH). YOU FAT WHORE!

GODFRIGH (*blubbers*). Take a hairy woman away from me! WILL YOU! ASK HER—THE HAIRY WOMAN WANTS TO BE WITH ME!

MARY (*crying*). O LEO, KEEP HIM AWAY FROM ME!

GODFRIGH. O HAIRY WOMAN, DON'T DENY ME! DON'T DENY ME!

MARY. O LEO, KEEP HIM AWAY!

LEO (*shielding* MARY). This woman does not want you, Frank!

GODFRIGH. COME HERE! COME HERE! COME HERE HAIRY WOMAN!

(ST. MARY OF EGYPT *enters.*)

ST. MARY.

> I am here, I am here, I was always here
> I was in the beginning and I am in the end
> I AM ALPHA AND OMEGA!

GODFRIGH (*runs to* ST. MARY). Two hairy women— but one loves me—one loves me!

ST. MARY. St. Mary loves the Christians, St. Mary hates the heathens, St. Mary of Egypt knows a Christian from a heathen.

GODFRIGH. I'M A CHRISTIAN, HAIRY WOMAN!

ST. MARY (*breathes heavy*). You're a Christian, son of Christ, Christ's son, fair-fleshed son of Christ! (*Sits down at table.*)

MARY (*To* ZOE). Want to be friends?

ZOE (*smiling*). We are always friends—come here and sit with me—and watch!

MARY (*she moves to* ZOE's *table*). I love to watch! (*Laughs.*)

ST. MARY. Pleasure, pleasure, pleasure from Christian men, one from the East (*Points to* LEO.) and one from the West! (*Points to* GODFRIGH.) Man from the East, man from the West! (*Laughs.*)

GODFRIGH. AND YOU WANT A MAN FROM THE WEST!

ST. MARY. I want what I want—CHRIST'S MAN- HOOD! Confess it! ONE OF YOU HAS IT! Which one is it, man from the East or man from the West!

LEO (*gently*). St. Mary has smoked too much hashish today.

ST. MARY. St. Mary of Egypt has smoked and the smoke has gone into her, LIKE THE SPIRIT OF CHRIST! THE SMOKE IN ME IS THE SPIRIT OF CHRIST! WHO WILL DENY THAT!

GODFRIGH. I DON'T DENY THAT—CHRIST WAS IN YOU! (*Laughs.*)

ST. MARY. ST. MARY HAD CHRIST IN HER TO THE FARTHEST END OF THE WORLD!

GODFRIGH (*laughing hard*). You're beautiful, Mary!

ST. MARY. St. Mary is beautiful, only the blind say naught, those with eyes see St. Mary of Egypt's beauty, those blessed with eyes can see the work of the Lord! I AM THE LORD'S WORK!

GODFRIGH. TELL THE MAN FROM THE EAST WHAT A GOOD FELLOW AM I!

ST. MARY (to LEO). Good—goodness sometimes comes from the far-off lands, the Lord is fair that way, he lets the goodness come over each part of the earth, spreading, spreading over, touching each of the Lord's creatures. The Lord's fair—he puts goodness into a man be he from the East or the West!

GODFRIGH (laughing). AND MAN PUTS GOODNESS INTO A WOMAN! I'VE PUT MY GOODNESS INTO ST. MARY!

LEO. You have put your hands on this woman! YOU HAVE CORRUPTED ONE OF GOD'S SAINTS!

GODFRIGH. MY NAME IS GODFRIGH! PUT THE LAST HALF OF MY NAME WHERE THE FIRST IS AND THE FIRST WHERE THE LAST IS! I FRIG GOD! (Laughs wild.)

LEO. You have debased our women—AND NOW YOU HAVE DARED TO DEBASE THE SAINTS OF OUR RELIGION!

GODFRIGH. I've had only one—ONE HAIRY WOMAN! ST. MARY OF EGYPT! The others don't like me—thank God for St. Mary of Egypt, who loves me!

ST. MARY. Thank God for St. Mary of Egypt—she who fled from the fierce Saracens—she who saved her purity from the ROTTENNESS OF SARACENS!

LEO. BUT YOU LET THIS FRANKISH-SWINE SPEW ON YOU! WHEN THE POPE'S MEN SPEW ON OUR SAINTS—THEY ARE SPEWING ON CHRIST! ST. MARY, HE SAID IT! HE SAID HE FRIGS GOD! WHY HAVE YOU LET HIM DEFILE YOU?

ST. MARY. Against me—my name—THERE IS NO DEFILEMENT! They rent Christ's robes—they swabbed Christ's lips with vinegar—YET THERE WAS NO DEFILEMENT! LIKE CHRIST I AM! AGAINST ME THERE IS NO DEFILEMENT!

LEO. BUT YOU CHOSE THIS STINKING DOG!

ST. MARY. I choose what I choose. It is no business of yours—would you say to Christ—CHRIST DO NOT CHOOSE ST. PETER!

LEO. BUT YOU ARE NOT CHRIST!

ST. MARY. I SHOULD CURSE YOU FOR THAT!

(*Everybody cringes, except* GODFRIGH.)

I SHOULD GIVE YOU THE EYE! (*Sticks out her fingers, gesture of a curse.*) I SHOULD MAKE YOUR TESTICLES WITHER AWAY! But I won't—dost thee desire me too? (*She squints, smiles cunningly.*)

LEO (*falls in front of her*). I DESIRE THEE TO LOVE ME LIKE A CHILD—AND PRAY FOR ME—O ST. MARY OF EGYPT—PRAY FOR ME—FORGIVE ME! DO NOT CURSE ME! FORGIVE ME!

ST. MARY (*smiling*). Ask the man from the West to forgive you—if he forgives you, St. Mary forgives you—if he forgives you—I WILL BLESS THEE!

LEO (*crying*). Curse me then.

ST. MARY. Thou art jealous of the man from the West! Jealous of St. Mary of Egypt! Jealous because of love! THEN VIE FOR ME, VIE FOR ME, FIGHT FOR ME —FIGHT LIKE CHRISTIANS FOR THE HOLY VESSEL! I AM THE VESSEL!

GODFRIGH. I don't want to fight—I'm tired. (*Lies down.*)

LEO (*hands* MARY OF EGYPT *nargileh*). Hashish, St. Mary of Egypt, smoke. I will dance. Mary and Zoe let's dance for St. Mary.

(*They dance.*)

ST. MARY. Hashish is good—I can dance better than those two—this hashish is good—I can dance better. (*She gets up, goes between the dancers, pipe in her mouth.*) SEE WHAT A WOMAN ST. MARY OF EGYPT IS! SHE CAN BLESS AND SHE CAN DANCE! Hashish is good—my lips on my pipe, my limbs moving, my hairshirt itching me, it gives me pleasure . . . Constantinople gives me pleasure. THE THREE OF YOU, WATCH! WATCH ST. MARY OF EGYPT DANCE!

(*They stop dancing and watch her.*)

AGAIN I SAY CONSTANTINOPLE GIVES ME PLEASURE! I PROTECT HER ALWAYS!—That's a good thing —I save Constantinople from SARACENS! SARACENS!

LECHERY! LECHEROUS SARACENS! AHHHHHHH
THE VISIONS! THE SUNSHINE ON THE DOME OF
ST. SOPHIA! IT SHARPENS THE IMAGE OF WHAT I
SEE—OF WHAT I SEE ON THE DOME OF BLESSED
ST. SOPHIA—I SEE BLACK LIPS—TERRIBLE BLACK
LIPS ON THE DOME—IT MEANS—THE BLACK LIPS
MEAN THE SARACENS! AHHHHHH SARACENS DE-
FILING ST. SOPHIA! SARACENS STEALING BEAU-
TIFUL ICONS, HOLY RELICS! AHHHHH I FEEL
THE STARE OF GOD ON ME NOW! CHRIST PAN-
TOCRATOR LOOKING DOWN ON ST. MARY OF
EGYPT! CHRIST PANTOCREATOR WANTS ST. MARY
OF EGYPT TO SAVE CONSTANTINOPLE FROM THE
SARACENS! AHHHHH I FEEL THE PAIN (*She falls.*)
THE PAIN OF CHRIST'S SORES—SARACENS ARE
STUFFING WOOL INTO CHRIST'S SORES—THE
WOOL REEKS WITH PISS! THEY ARE TEARING
CHRIST'S BODY UP WITH THEIR TEETH! AHHHHH
ST. MARY OF EGYPT MUST STOP THEM—MUST
STOP THEM FROM BITING CHRIST! CONSTANTI-
NOPLE MUST BE SAVED!

> (MARY, ZOE, LEO *look confused, anxious. They leave,*
> ROBED MAN *looks at* ST. MARY *and leaves, she lies*
> *still for awhile.*)

I smell them, I smell the Saracens, sons-of-bitches, blood-
suckers—they have sucked Christ's blood up—his blood
turns black in their mouths. (*She sits up, sees* GODFRIGH.)
HERE IS ONE! HERE IS A SARACEN! (*She circles*
him.) PRETENDING TO BE ASLEEP—LIKE EGYPT
PRETENDS THAT GOD NEVER CURSED HER! I'M
NOT UNSEEING! ST. MARY OF EGYPT SEES! HOR-
RIBLE SARACEN! YOU WILL NOT RUIN CONSTAN-
TINOPLE! I'LL SQUEEZE GALL AND BILE OUT OF
YOU! SQUEEZE YOU LIKE THE NECK OF A GOOSE!
AHHHHH ST. MARY OF EGYPT'S FACE BURNS! IS
THE SUN SHINING ON IT? (*Her teeth chatter.*) MY
TEETH ARE CLACKING! THE SARACEN IS DOING
IT! HE IS MAKING ME BURN! LORD, HOW DO I—
HOW DO I KILL BARABBAS? AHHHHH MY LEGS
BURN! MY LEGS BURN! LEG—It is a sign—I MUST
CUT OFF THE SARACEN'S LEG—EVIL—THE LEG
IS EVIL—IF I CUT OFF HIS—MINE WILL BE COOL!

(*Music plays loud, lights dim,* MARY *crouches over*
GODFRIGH *with knife, swipes at him. He screams.*)
I AM COOL!

SCENE V

(ALICE *and* LEO *are in bed in an embrace.*)

ALICE. Now say it slowly, s-l-o-w-l-y.

LEO. Godfrigh is dead.

ALICE. I'm embarrassed.

LEO. Embarrassed?

ALICE. Well . . . Godfrigh is dead . . . killed by an
ugly woman. It's embarrassing . . . because I'm beautiful.
(*Stretches out leg and looks at it, donkey-laughs.*)

LEO. The woman is a saint—and don't laugh like that.

ALICE. A woman killed my husband—and I laugh that
way because I'm NERVOUS! I loved Godfrigh.

LEO. He didn't know how to love you . . .

ALICE. O STOP IT—YOU DON'T KNOW ANYTHING
ABOUT IT. I DON'T WANT TO TALK ABOUT IT—
him—like this—but I must. Turn over and look the other
way—DON'T LOOK AT ME!

LEO. Turn over—don't look at you—what . . .

ALICE. Please—MY HUSBAND IS DEAD!—Do what
I ask of you. I want to feel you near me—but I want to
talk—O I'M ASKING YOU TO MOVE OVER—and look
the other way!

LEO (*tired*). Yes—I understand you. (*He turns away.*)

ALICE. He liked this woman . . . the saint . . . to him
she was more perfect than me . . . I am conceited . . .
yes, Leo . . . but don't answer me . . . I am conceited
. . . the woman cut his leg off . . . amputated his leg . . .
in amputation . . . there is collapse . . . a damage . . .
she made mincemeat out of him . . . Godfrigh. She has
thick hair . . . St. Mary of Egypt . . . St. Mary's fingers
were studded with blood . . . STUDDED—LEO, YOU
ARE MY STUD! AND GODFRIGH IS DEAD!

(LEO *grumbles.*)

In Normandy we were privileged . . . and here . . . CON-
STANTINOPLE IS FILLED WITH BAD AIR! Harm,
that is what I've had in Constantinople. Godfrigh's body
is stiff now . . . his one leg is probably quite stiff . . .
fantastic! Godfrigh drooled for the woman . . . one day
I'll be toothless and I'll drool—and then I'll remember how

Godfrigh drooled for a woman—not me—an Eastern woman —a saint . . . perhaps then, without my teeth . . . I will be sweeter and gentler. It's vexing—hot, false Constantinople . . . we were deceived. Godfrigh's body will decay . . . the worms—the parasitic worms will be full of his blood—maybe wine—he drank a lot of wine—(*To* LEO.) WORMS WILL DRINK HIS WINE! Mercy, lovingness, CHRIST—give mercy and lovingness to Godfrigh—I never did. (*Crying.*) Leo, will you go with me to Normandy? I want you!

LEO. I can't.

ALICE. YOU MUST! I NEED YOU . . . A husband . . .

LEO. You'll get a husband again . . . but not me.

ALICE. Don't you love me?

LEO. No, my Alice . . . no. (*Wisely.*) And you don't care.

ALICE. YES—I DO—I DO!

LEO. No, you don't.

ALICE. You're right . . . I don't . . . You wouldn't be happy in Normandy—you would be full of sorrow there . . . like I am here in Constantinople—IT MADE US GREEDY—GOLD EVERYWHERE—in hot Constantinople—they even make Christ's eyes gold! Ecstasy . . . bloodpoison . . . it's all here—why do you want to stay, Leo?

LEO. Constantinople? Because I love it. You know, Alice—you have the smoothest, silkiest skin—we have only one hour (*Laughs.*) before the Saracens come.

ALICE. Saracens come? This is the first time I've heard —is it true—are the Saracens coming?

LEO. Umhummmm. (*He kisses her.*)

THE LIFE OF LADY GODIVA

an hysterical drama

Ronald Tavel

Playbill for Premiere Production

THE LIFE OF LADY GODIVA

an hysterical drama by Ronald Tavel
Presented at Theater of the Ridiculous
(New York City)

"We have passed beyond the absurd: our position
is absolutely preposterous"
—Ronald Tavel

Directed by John Vaccaro

CAST IN ORDER OF APPEARANCE

NUNS' CHORUS....Regina Hirsch, Sister Flossie of the Cross,
     Mario Montez, Heller Grace, Margit Winckler
MOTHER SUPERVIVA ....John Vaccaro
LADY GODIVA ....Dorothy Opalach
TOM ....Charles Ludlam
KASHA VERONICAS ....Elsene Sorrentino
THOROLD ....Dashwood von Blocksburg
EARL LEOFFRIC ....Tom Shibona
Set designs: L. L. Powers
Set: L. L. Powers, J. D. Greenstein
Lighting: Bill Walters
Costume designs: Jack Smith
Costumes: Fran & Flo
Horse: Joseph Peroni
Graphic design: L. L. Powers
Imprimeur: Peter Birnbaum

Music: Franz Liszt, John Vaccaro
Stage manager: Richard Kohn
Assistants: Michael Manns, Larry Rutter
Regisseur: Harvey Tavel

———————

RONALD TAVEL

"I was born near Gravesend Bay and raised in the Bath Beach section of Brooklyn. Bearing a Swiss-Huguenot name, my family actually derives from over a half dozen countries of Europe and Asia. After leaving the universities (where I majored in Philosophy and Literature) I traveled in Canada, Mexico, Cuba, France, and Spain. My strange and often terrifying experiences during a prolonged sojourn in Africa became the background for my lengthy novel *Street of Stairs* (sections of which appear in various issues of *The Chicago Review* and *Intransit*).

"I have been playwright-in-residence of the Theater of the Ridiculous which produced such plays of mine as *Shower*, *The Life of Juanita Castro*, *The Life of Lady Godiva*, *Screen Test*, *Indira Gandhi's Daring Device*, and *Kitchenette*. I am also Andy Warhol's scenarist, having written the screenplays for almost a score of movies, among them *The Chelsea Girls*, *Horse*, *Vinyl*, and *Hedy*. My dramatic writings are published in *Partisan Review*, *Clyde*, *Blacklist*, *Tri-Quarterly*, and *Film Culture*. My essays appear in *The New American Cinema* (E. P. Dutton & Co.), *Aspen*, and *Graffiti;* my poetry in *The Chicago Review*, *Wormwood*, *Tri-Quarterly*, etc. I am the author of the Judson Memorial Church production of *Gorilla Queen*."

(Curtain, dark stage. Silence. Then a strong spotlight illuminates a very long chaise longue somewhat left of center. A small end table about 2½ ft. high near the chaise, with a bottle of soda pop, a glass, an ashtray, a pack of long cigarettes on it, a Tiffany lamp suspended from above. Unless otherwise specified, the decor and costumes should be in Art Nouveau style. MOTHER SUPERVIVA *is discovered sitting in the direct center of the chaise; she is sitting up very stiff and proper, severe.* SUPERVIVA *is played by a male actor.* SUPERVIVA *is dressed in an English fin de siècle type nun's habit, with brimming hood, white bib and blue gown.)*

SUPERVIVA. You will discover that from this point on, every line is better than the next.

(A very long pause. SUPERVIVA *extracts a cigarette from the pack on the table, lights it in a long cigarette holder, and stretches herself out full length on the chaise longue.)*

Nudity is the quintessence of essence, though it is sick-rilegious to say so . . . *(Long pause.)* Nudity is the most natural prerogative of the innovational spirit.

(The spotlight weakens on SUPERVIVA *smoking luxuriantly and flicking ashes and at this point the overture starts. It should be Art Nouveau music; if original music is not available, the end of Liszt's "Les Préludes" should be used. A strong spot lights upstage center. A sheer curtain with peacock feather and tendril designs is hanging there, and through it we can see a wooden white horse. The horse's body is very long, more than twice the length it should be.* TOM *is seated far up near the horse's neck, while* LADY GODIVA *is planted on the horse's rump.* TOM *is dressed with cap and jacket like a taxi driver. He*

*has a coin changer strapped around his waist and
dangling over his crotch. There is a steering wheel
coming up from the base of the horse's neck, a rear-
view mirror coming out from its head, and a brake
coming up from its side; gas pedal also on the
flank.* TOM *has both his hands on the steering
wheel.* GODIVA, *a buxom beauty, is dressed in a
Gibson Girl gown with lace-collar coming up to her
chin; Gibson Girl hair-do. Both sit for a tableau
vivant until the overture finishes. Then they both
speak with exaggerated British accents.*)

GODIVA (*laughing*). Did you say big? Why, my dear,
it was one of the pillars of civilization!!

TOM. And then what happened?

GODIVA. Then when?

TOM. When there was nothing else left to pull off?

GODIVA. Why, then we pulled off the curtains—and let
the sunlight in!!

(*Both laugh. Long pause.* GODIVA *takes out her lipstick and begins to apply it.* TOM *adjusts the rear-
view mirror so that he can watch her.* GODIVA *ap-
plies the lipstick vulgarly.* TOM *stares harder into
the mirror. At this point* TOM *speaks with a heavy
Mexican accent and* GODIVA *speaks English or Span-
ish with a very thick Brooklyn accent.*)

(*Suggestively.*) Yo may yamo Rosita . . . (*Sexy pause.*)
Deesay!—Rosita!—deesay!

TOM (*clumsy*). Rosita.

GODIVA. Bu-ay-no! . . . Rosita Schwartzberger. Deesay!

TOM. Rosita Hamberger.

GODIVA. No! no! Schwartzberger! Schwartzberger! Rosita Schwartzberger. Deesay! Deesay!

TOM. Rosita Shortsbugger.

GODIVA. Correcto! Como say yamo?

TOM. Me Tom. Me Tom da cabbie.

GODIVA. Hi ya, Tom.

(GODIVA *continues to apply her lipstick.* TOM *stares
madly into the mirror.* GODIVA *begins to lift the
skirt of her gown slightly, exposing her ankle.* TOM
*adjusts the mirror so that he can view her limb. He
neglects his steering, seems nearly to crash head-on,
swerves, they both get jolted.* GODIVA *recoups, re-*

sumes her suggestive lipstick application with one hand, continues to lift her hem with the other.)

Soy professor day English . . .

TOM *(slowly, beginning to catch on).* Si?

GODIVA. Si. Ke-air-ays kay tay day classes in English?

TOM *(slowly).* Si . . . como no?

GODIVA. Bu-ay-no. Yo resto a Hotel Hilton. Nonyona por la monyana es buy-ay-no?

TOM. Si.

GODIVA. Moy bu-ay-no, Señor Tom Taxi-driver. *(Puts away her cosmetic, straightens her gown, and carefully gets off the horse's behind, carefully making the most, in doing so, of her own behind and other ample charms. Patting the horse's behind.)* That's what I call a real rumpseat, honey. *(To* TOM.*)* Oh, Señor Taxi-Driver, es nesssess-serio a pagar?

TOM. A . . . a . . . no.

GODIVA. That's what I thought. Thanks, honey, see ya later. Sucker.

> *(*TOM *remains seated on the horse and continues to steer. At this point the* NUNS' CHORUS *bursts into a choral background accompaniment.)*

CHORUS *(singing).*

> Guadalahooer! Guadalahooer!

(The CHORUS *keeps up this single word accompaniment to the tune of "Guadalajara."* GODIVA *comes through the center of the curtains and sings the following song. If original music is not available she should sing to the tune of "Darling, I Am Growing Old.")*

GODIVA *(singing).*

Darling, I am growing thin!
I have lost my double chin.
I'm not what I might have been.
Had I really learned to sin.

Darling, I feel kind of ill,
My physique is next to nil:
I seem short of verve and will—
Sex don't gimme no more thrill.

So rich knight and stately earl

Keep your diamond broach and pearl,
I'll no longer hump and swirl
—And that's why they call me the Gibson Girl!

(*The* CHORUS *dies out as* GODIVA *moves forward
downstage.*)

Hello? Hello? Anybody here? Yoo-hoo!! What a joint.
Dead as the morgue.

(SISTER KASHA VERONICAS *comes hobbling on from
right, sweet old thing, a bit out of breath. She is
in English* fin de siècle *nun's habit, with a cobbler's
apron around her waist. She carries a candle.*)

VERONICAS. Coming, I'm coming. Just a moment,
please.

GODIVA (*cheap*). Hi!

VERONICAS. Good day, my dear, what can I do for
you?

GODIVA (*tough*). I don't know yet.

VERONICAS (*sweetly*). Well, my child, can I help you?

GODIVA. I don't know. Can you?

VERONICAS. I don't know. Won't you let me try?

GODIVA. Why don't you *try* on someone else! I'm looking for the Luz convent.

VERONICAS. This is a loose convent. Won't you come
in?

(*They step into* SUPERVIVA's *spotlight.* VERONICAS
brings the candle close to GODIVA's *face.*)

Oh, my goodness, what are those bags under your eyes?

GODIVA. They're my Saratoga trunks. I'm traveling
light.

VERONICAS. Oh, I see. Now: how can I help you?

GODIVA. Well, for one thing, I need new soles on
these oxfords. (*Taking off her shoes and handing them to*
VERONICAS.)

VERONICAS (*looking down at* GODIVA's *bare feet*). Oh, I
see you're going to want one-day service. Won't you
please have a seat while you're waiting?

(VERONICAS *roughl yshoves* SUPERVIVA *aside and she
and* GODIVA *sit on the chaise to the right of* SUPER-
VIVA. VERONICAS *takes hammer and nails and new
soles from her cobbler's apron and begins working
on the shoes.* GODIVA *squats cheaply, like an un-*

comfortable whore. Both do not acknowledge the
presence of SUPERVIVA.)

SUPERVIVA (*a little annoyed*). Mayor Wagner does it.

VERONICAS (*without looking up from her work*). How do you know?

SUPERVIVA. Because he had to get married again.

GODIVA. Boy, am I fagged.

VERONICAS. Been burning your bottom—I mean—your candle at both ends again, my child?

GODIVA. Well, I don't want to bore you with another wayside tale, but on my way here I stopped off for a minute and went into the bushes for an occasion, and it turned into an event.

SUPERVIVA. Some wayside tale: sounds more like a waylaid tail.

VERONICAS. Well, now, that wasn't so smart of you, was it, to go into the bushes all alone like that?

GODIVA. I know I ain't so smart. But brains aren't everything. A good pair of walking shoes can get you just as far in life.

VERONICAS. Of course, dear, and I'll have these oxfords soled for you in just two shakes of a bunny's tail.

GODIVA. I don't think I caught your name, honey.

VERONICAS (cute). Oh-no! that's because it's not contagious.

SUPERVIVA (*sour*). Which is about all of her that's not.

VERONICAS. I am Sister Kasha Veronicas.

SUPERVIVA. The department of health, education and welfare wishes to acquaint you both with lymphogranuloma venereum. A venerable disease, to be sure.

GODIVA. Who's the old lady?

VERONICAS. Oh, that's Mother Superviva. She is the mother of all us sisters here at the convent.

GODIVA. I'm glad to meet a mother, anytime. My own died when she was struck by lightning, you know.

VERONICAS (*sweetly*). Well, if you have to go, it's nice to go quickly like that, isn't it?

SUPERVIVA. All persons with genital lesions should have a darkfield examination to rule out the possibility of mixed infections. Nothing is so necessary in blue-blood society as a pure contamination.

GODIVA. Bushes or no bushes, I'll skip the darkfield examination, if you don't mind.

SUPERVIVA. But it is best to be sure. If you can't be sure, at least you can be uncertain. It is best to be uncertain. Yes, I am certain.

VERONICAS (*very busy at the shoes*). Its main manifestation in tropical areas is yaws. What's yaws is mine.

SUPERVIVA. Sister Kasha Veronicas, don't you have the dishes to do? Remember—keep America clean!

VERONICAS (*flustered*). I have dishing to do, strictly clean, but Mother Superviva, I haven't completed cobbling these oxfords.

SUPERVIVA. How dare you talk back to me! I'd watch my step if I were you! I would remember the Maine, I would remember the Alamo and 44-69 or fight, if I were you!!! Now, get off this set!

VERONICAS (*cowed*). Oh, forgive me, Mother, I am not wholly responsible for the sounds that issue from me.

SUPERVIVA. Issue those sounds in your private quarters!

GODIVA. Or from your private quarters.

SUPERVIVA. Sister Kasha Veronicas, begone!

(VERONICAS *hobbles upstage, muttering in bitterness for being scolded at, and goes through the sheer curtain. She seats herself under the horse's belly and continues to hammer away at the shoe repairing. During the following scene, something seems to go wrong with the mechanism of the horse and* TOM *has trouble with the brake and pedal. He dismounts and examines for the trouble in the horse's mouth, in its rear end, and notably its pendant sex which he cranks like a jack.* VERONICAS *works away unnoticing during all this, but when* TOM *is down beside her cranking, they take notice of each other, begin to get familiar.*

As soon as VERONICAS *leaves the chaise, a change comes over* GODIVA: *she throws herself at the feet of* SUPERVIVA *and pleads desperately. She will speak in her natural voice from this point on.*)

GODIVA. Please, please, Mother Superviva, I beg of you, let me take my final vows now!!!

SUPERVIVA (*bending over, quickly*). First tell us who drugged Sister Kasha Veronicas!

GODIVA (*puzzled*). Who drugged Kasha Veronicas? Is she drugged?

SUPERVIVA. Hooer, you!

GODIVA. Who am I? I am Godiva. Lady Godiva.

SUPERVIVA. Lady, huh? Never knew the hooer who didn't claim she was a lady.

GODIVA. But I *am* a lady. I am Lady Godiva. Don't you believe me?

SUPERVIVA. Certainly not! I never believed that horse maneuver about Lady Godiva. So far as I'm concerned, it's all just a symbolic tale. Godiva divested herself symbolically: i.e., she stripped herself of her superfluous jewels in order to pay the levied tax.

GODIVA. You'll find my tail (*Swishing her rump.*) is not all that symbolic! Just wait and see.

SUPERVIVA (*in a deep masculine voice, suddenly very lecherously masculine*). As a matter of fact, I am actually quite interested in pursuing my studies on the historical subject. (*Appraising her physically.*) I *do* have an open mind: I should be more than willing to draw new conclusions at the presentation of convincing facts.

GODIVA. You'll be able to draw and conclude in good time: only, please, I implore you, let me take my final vows now.

SUPERVIVA. What unambiguous temerity! How sickrilegious of a person of your profession to insist upon the vows! Where's your religious background, my child?

GODIVA. In the background, that's for sure. (*Singing.*) "And that's why they call me the Gibson Girl . . ."

VERONICAS. Kochel listing 2–4–69.

SUPERVIVA. Spare us the vocal specialties, canary, and just tell me what you've been doing to merit the veil.

GODIVA (*sadly*). These days I really can't say I've been doing anyone—I mean anything,—except despairing.

SUPERVIVA. How nineteen fiftyish of you!

GODIVA (*wickedly, Brooklyn accent again*). Yeah, but you shoulda seen what I was doing in the nineteen fifties!

SUPERVIVA. Well, Madam Godiva, before I commit myself any further, you'll have to undergo a federal in-

vestigation. (*She blows out the candle on the table.*) Sister
Kasha Veronicas!

> (VERONICAS *is startled out of her intimacies with* TOM.
> *She breaks with frustration and adjusts her gown.*)

VERONICAS. Coming, Mother!

TOM. Coming down.

SUPERVIVA. Kindly desist from coming! Go and fetch
me Thorold the Sheriff.

VERONICAS. For your—I mean—at your service, Mother.
(*To* TOM.) You really don't have very many lines, do you,
sweetie?

TOM. I guess I don't. You see, I'm still being groomed
for stardom.

VERONICAS. Well, hang on, sweetie, I'm sure you'll
make it.

TOM. Bye bye, bouncy.

> (VERONICAS *goes out left.* TOM *sits twiddling his*
> *thumbs for a while and then resumes twiddling*
> *with the horse.*)

SUPERVIVA. Care for a drink, Lady, while we're waiting for the Sheriff?

GODIVA. Well, I hardly ever implode.

SUPERVIVA. But are often implode*d*, I'll wager.

> (GODIVA *and* SUPERVIVA *sit suggestively together on*
> *the chaise longue, and* SUPERVIVA *pours a drink*
> *from the soda pop bottle into a glass. She lights a*
> *cigarette and hands the glass to* GODIVA.)

Here's shit in your face, honey.

GODIVA. Thanks, Mother. (*She takes a small sip; an*
ambiguous expression awakens on her face.) Er—what is it?

SUPERVIVA. It's celery tonic. Don't you like it?

GODIVA. Well, the taste is very Art Nouveau. (*She*
holds her nose and drains off the glass.)

SUPERVIVA. You certainly drank that quickly enough.

GODIVA. With some things, the sooner they're over,
the better.

> (SUPERVIVA *edges a little closer to* GODIVA. *She is*
> *dragging deliciously on her cigarette.* GODIVA
> *squirms somewhat uneasily, confused by the deep*
> *voice and masculine aggressiveness of* SUPERVIVA.)

There's a quarter in it for you if you can douse that
cigarette without burning me.

SUPERVIVA. What are you implying?

GODIVA. I'm implying nothing. Burn a hole in my new Gibson Girl dress and I'll slap you with a fifty dollar bill.

SUPERVIVA. If you have one! (*Pulling away, now very defensive.*) Just so there's no confusion, my dear, let me repeat: I am the woman of the dunes. (*She clasps both hands on her falsies. Then she brings them forward and places her bosom on the table top.*) And I rest my case!

(*A flourish.* VERONICAS *re-enters downstage left with* THOROLD THE SHERIFF. *He is dressed in medieval sheriff garb.*)

VERONICAS. Announcing Thorold, oldest sheriff in Warwickshire; His Majesty's vice-squad viceroy to Coventry!

THOROLD. Chuck the fanfare, baby, I'm here on Fed business.

SUPERVIVA (*rushing up to* THOROLD *and kissing him*). Good Thorold, cast thy nighted business color off and let thine eye look like a friend on Coventry. Do not forever with thy veiled lids seek for thy noble—

THOROLD. Chuck the fanfare, Mother, I'm representing the law now, and the law can have no friends, much less filial feeling. (*Feeling* SUPERVIVA *familiarly, of course.*)

SUPERVIVA (*enthralled*). My son, the Sheriff! So official!

THOROLD (*to* GODIVA). Stand up, young lady!

GODIVA (*jumping up*). Young Lady Godiva, sir!

THOROLD. No back-talk. How do you expect me to investigate you with that Gibson gown on?

GODIVA (*humbly*). I bought it big, sir, so it would be good for next year.

THOROLD. A chestful of frugality. Fill me in on your particulars.

GODIVA. They're hard to fill in, sir. I wanted to be a Playboy bunny. I wanted to be a bunny boys play with. A hundred times I filled out applications. (*Indicating her breasts.*) But the personnel department said there was nothing left for the imagination to fill in, and failed to hire me.

THOROLD (*coming on to her*). You have nothing to lose being a bunny . . . except tail.

GODIVA (*whorish again, Brooklyn accent*). I'm a two-time loser. So what's your pitch, copper?

SUPERVIVA. With two balls and no fouls you've got a strike. But tell her yourself, son.

VERONICAS. Yeah, Thor, tell the dearie.

TOM. Tell her, tell her good, Thorold!

VERONICAS. He must have improvised that line.

GODIVA. Well, Mr. Sheriff, I'm all ears.

THOROLD. I see you have a sense of English understatement.

SUPERVIVA. Thorold, I'd like to see you in my closet.

THOROLD. You've got the wrong play, madam.

GODIVA. I said I'm waiting, Mr. Sheriff. What's the pitch?

THOROLD (*taking* GODIVA *around the shoulder*). O.K., baby, here's the pitch: and listen carefully 'cause I'm only gonna tell you once. Also, this is the exposition, so if you don't get it now, you're screwed, dig?

GODIVA. Shoot.

THOROLD. It seems this guy, Leofric (*Pronounced Leffric.*) Goodrich, has recently levied such a heavy tax on the local inhabitants that nobody can afford to patronize this establishment. You hip? Now, it's your job to charm this Leofric into remitting the tax so this business can get back on its back—I mean, on its feet.

GODIVA. What's in it for me?

THOROLD. You pull this off and you can take the veil.

GODIVA. I don't believe you.

THOROLD. Have you ever known me to lie, Lady Godiva?

GODIVA. No, never.

THOROLD. Well, there's always a first time.

SUPERVIVA (*in heavy exotic accent*). Listen to him: he tells you the truth. He is not just standing around here waiting for a bus.

GODIVA. But how can you ask *me* to engage in such an enterprise? I am an artist. How can an artist forget about her art?

VERONICAS. Easy. Just put an "F" in front of it.

SUPERVIVA (*her conscience getting to her*). Pity we have to resort to these deceptions. Still, at any rate, it's a good thing hooers can't think and don't have feelings.

*(Suddenly a strong spotlight falls on upstage right.
A grand flourish. We see LEOFRIC GOODRICH standing there, snarling. LEOFRIC is a bearded, tall, dark
and handsome leading man, dressed in sado-maso-
chist leather outfit from head to toe. He carries a
long whip which he brandishes and cracks im-
pressively. Everyone turns toward him.)*

VERONICAS. Announcing Leofric Goodrich, Earl of
Mercia, Lord of Castle Coventry in Warwickshire, de-
spoiler of the poor, divester of the tithes, and do-badder
for Edward the Confessor, or so the latter hath confessed!

THOROLD. The very stud in question—go to it, Godiva!

VERONICAS. Good luck, Godiva girl!

SUPERVIVA. Con the convent's prosperity, my child, our
future hangs upon your hips.

*(There is a chaotic scurrying for position: SUPERVIVA
and THOROLD sit on the right end of the chaise and
embrace rather Oedipally, mother and son. VERONI-
CAS sits on the left end of the chaise. A space is
left in the center where LEOFRIC and GODIVA will
soon squeeze themselves in. Their lovemaking will
constantly squash up against VERONICAS and
threaten to throw her off the left edge. TOM mounts
the horse in a single bound and steers madly.*

*For the moment, LEOFRIC comes rushing fiercely
downstage and seizes GODIVA by the arm. He cracks
his whip.)*

LEOFRIC. Ah-ha! my luscious, irresistibly lovely buxom
box! You must be a lot of fun—with a little less fat.

GODIVA. Why do you grab me?—I won't run away.

LEOFRIC. When you find out what I am going to do to
you, you will!

GODIVA. Je veux être vedette. *[Pronounced Je veuet
vedet.]*

LEOFRIC. Never knew the hooer who didn't make some
such claim. But a hooer is a hooer is a hooer is a hooer!

VERONICAS. Even if it *is* true, a gentleman doesn't
say so.

LEOFRIC. Silence! No one has asked for your opinion.

VERONICAS. No one ever does.

LEOFRIC. What's your name, baby?

GODIVA (*with heavy exotic accent*). Men, in their foolishness, gif me the name which means "beautiful."

LEOFRIC. In their foolishness??—in their blindness, you mean. Get on the couch!

(LEFORIC *tosses* GODIVA *on the chaise and attempts to mount her.* VERONICAS *nearly gets thrown off.*)

VERONICAS. What the heck? And I got here early just to be assured of a good seat.

THOROLD (*hugging* SUPERVIVA). I'm glad we decided on the back row, aren't you, Mamma?

SUPERVIVA. Hmmmmm . . . sonny boy . . .

(GODIVA *struggles out from under* LEOFRIC, *desperately adjusting her collar and hair-do.*)

GODIVA. Er, er—care for a drink?

LEOFRIC. If it's good and dry—and I'll stray lower where the real martinis lie.

GODIVA. That's a manhattan down below . . . (*Winking at him.*) if you catch my meaning . . .

VERONICAS. Some of the people you can fool all of the time.

SUPERVIVA. And some just when it suits the rhyme.

(GODIVA *pours a drink from the soda pop bottle and hands the glass to* LEOFRIC. VERONICAS *resumes cobbling the shoes.*)

GODIVA. Here's shit in your face, honey.

LEOFRIC. Thanks, hooer. (*He takes a small sip; an ambiguous expression awakens on his face.*) Er—what is it?

GODIVA. It's celery tonic. Don't you like it?

LEOFRIC. Well, the taste is very Art Nouveau. (*He grabs his crotch and drains off the glass.*)

GODIVA. You certainly drank that quickly enough.

LEOFRIC. With some things, the sooner they're over, the better. And you better taste better than this!

GODIVA. What makes you think you're even in a position to judge?

VERONICAS. Position is everything in life.

LEOFRIC. Because I have good taste.

SUPERVIVA. So he claims. But scratch an American deep enough and you'll find a Philistine.

VERONICAS. Oh, I'll bet he has good taste and tastes good, too.

LEOFRIC. What's your line of business, baby?

GODIVA. I'm in the clothes line.

VERONICAS. A clothesline. How sweet. Yet dry. (*Hammering at the shoes.*) I'll have these hoofers soled in just the shake of two tails. Our repair policy: "Sex While You Wait."

GODIVA. Actually, Leofric, I'm a fashion model.

THOROLD. Seems to me Godiva would have more success as a calendar model.

> (GODIVA *gets up and takes a model's stroll across the stage. Model music is heard in the background, counterpointed by the* NUNS' CHORUS *singing softly,* "Guadalahooer, Guadalahooer.")

GODIVA. About this heat-wave time we start exhibiting our exciting new virginsfall creations. We're stressing virgin olive-oil wool fashions for great-great-grandmothers. The high price of the wares is intended to compensate for the limited market.

THOROLD. Imagine that: new fashion trends for virgin grandmothers by Lady Godiva of Coventry!

VERONICAS (*paranoid*). Wonder what he meant by that?

LEOFRIC. I'd like to see your wares for a hotter climate: like Bangkok—or Bumppussy.

> (LEOFRIC *leaps up, seizes* GODIVA, *and hurls her back on the chaise.* VERONICAS *is shoved, by the action, to the floor.*)

Oh, Montana Mush! you're something I could really get my fingers lost in!

> (LEOFRIC *falls to his knees and throws up the skirts of* GODIVA's *dress. He kisses her bare feet savagely. She giggles.* TOM *giggles in unison. Then* LEOFRIC *pulls away suddenly and examines the bottoms of* GODIVA's *feet.*)

Ever notice how much the sole is like the palm?

GODIVA. What are you doing—reading my future?

LEOFRIC. Yeah, I see a peace march in your future.

GODIVA. Wrong:—it'll be a ride.

> (LEOFRIC *crawls up her legs, giving them a thorough investigation. But he loses his fierceness as he rises and waxes unexpectedly romantic.* VERONICAS *is sentimentally touched by proxy;* THOROLD *and* SU-PERVIVA *too involved to notice right now.*)

LEOFRIC. Ever have a lover before with a beard?

GODIVA. Yes.

LEOFRIC. Oh, you jade!—even that you've had.

GODIVA. Well . . . it's the neighborhood.

VERONICAS (*swooning*). Coventry's left bank!

GODIVA. I'd like to see you shave that beard, Leofric. I mean, so I can see what you really look like.

LEOFRIC. How ridiculous! Shall I shave that dog or that pussy or that bunny or that wooden horse's mane and tail so you can see what they really look like??!! This *is* what I really look like. *You* are not what you really look like.

GODIVA. I assure you, I ain't the bearded lady.

SUPERVIVA. Yeah, she ain't. But might be one or two here not so free from suspicion.

THOROLD (*giving* SUPERVIVA *a phial*). Here, have some Ban, Mother, it takes the worry out of being close.

> (LEOFRIC's *hand has entered the exhausted* GODIVA's *bosom.*)

GODIVA. What *are* you doing?

LEOFRIC. Mean to tell me you don't know?

GODIVA. Have you ever read folk tales of Malaysia, Leofric?

LEOFRIC. Yes.

GODIVA. What?

LEOFRIC (*annoyed*). "Yam."

VERONICAS. How successfully she fends him off. It's very much like being in the Poconos.

SUPERVIVA. In the what?

THOROLD. Poke whose nose! I'm the law around here.

LEOFRIC (*hot and bothered*). Listen, give me an heir, or I'll give you the air!

GODIVA. That's just letting the fart from a loftier locale.

VERONICAS. That line was banned from an earlier version of this scene—to take the worry out of being close.

THOROLD. Hey, Godiva, you've worked his wanter up enough. You can spring the proposition now.

LEOFRIC. Who the hell are you?

THOROLD. I'm Thorold, Godiva's press agent.

SUPERVIVA. My son, the press agent!

LEOFRIC. Your son no less, and a press agent!

THOROLD. Make with the proposition, Godiva.

LEOFRIC. What proposition? What's this about a proposition?

SUPERVIVA. Go ahead, Godiva.

GODIVA. Listen, Leofric dear: are you really a virgin vampire? I mean, that is to say, do you really have a yen for that manhattan lying low?

LEOFRIC *(pulling away)*. What of it?

VERONICAS. Ooooooo—it's all so exciting!

GODIVA. Well, I didn't have the heart to tell you before, but you see, there's a string attached.

LEOFRIC. There's a lot of lace and bodice and crinoline and girdle and leggings too.—O.K., Miss Plumply Teasing, what's the string?

> *(A noisy, melodramatic snatch of trumpetry from "Les Préludes" is heard.* LEOFRIC *stands up to his full fearsome height.* GODIVA *goes down on her knees before him.* SUPERVIVA, THOROLD *and* VERONICAS *go down on their knees.* TOM *goes down on his knees, supplicating before the horse's pendant crank.* TOM *assumes the exact same kneeling position, angle, etc., as* GODIVA.*)*

GODIVA. O, beneficent Leofric, good and rich, Earl of Mercia and most merciful, moveable Master of Castle Coventry and O worshipful Ward of Warwickshire, O remit the heavy duty that thou hast laid upon the peasantrie in the hereabouts, that thereby relieved they might come hither to this house and further relieve themselves. Do thou this in remembrance of thine own lecheries. We four supplicate thee, then, for this.

THE FOUR. Amen!

TOM. Ah women!

> *(LEOFRIC stands motionless for a moment, puzzled. Everything hangs in suspension. He comes very slowly forward downstage. He pauses dramatically. Then he undoes his garrison buckle, lets down his leather trousers, adjusts his leather shirt, and zips up his fly again and fixes his buckle.)*

THOROLD. Hey, Leofric, you wanna take that bit on tour?

SUPERVIVA. My son, the press agent!

LEOFRIC *(the height of drama)*. Ah, always and again there are strings attached. Authority is post-dated. Shall

I reign forever in Mercia and never be understood? Is it too much to ask that my every decree, my every gesture be studied? How can you claim to serve me unless you comprehend the manner in which I pick up a pretzel after taking a sip of celery tonic?

TOM (*poking his head through the sheer curtain*). James Dean is dead!

SUPERVIVA (*sadly*). Ah, well, one less mouth to feed.

(LEOFRIC *walks slowly back to* GODIVA *and lifts her to her feet.* TOM *rises with the self-same motion.*)

LEOFRIC. What did you say your name was, my child?

GODIVA. Godiva.

LEOFRIC. Ah, Godiva. Lady Godiva. Then it is clear, my child, what you must do. And my duty is clear too, the demand I must make is clear. For all this was written in the mind of God and thereafter inscribed in the history books long before either of us was born. And all these things I re-rehearse in you that that which happens in the future may be closer to you.

TOM. Oh, go on and tell her already.

LEOFRIC. Lady Godiva:—you must

THOROLD. Ride through the market place of Coventry

VERONICAS. At high noon

TOM. On the back of this old horse

SUPERVIVA. Stark naked!

LEOFRIC. And on that condition only can I remit the tax. You see, you were right, you were all right, you of this house against itself and me:—There are always strings attached.

VERONICAS (*very low*). Even if it is true, gentleman playwrights don't say so . . .

(*A long pause. Everyone on stage maintains his position a little uneasily as if not knowing what to do next; as if there were really nothing to do next.*)

LEOFRIC (*unsure of himself*). Godiva, lay this rhyme to thy heart, by way of consolation: When the Queen rides from her den, so, too, ride all her men.

(*Another long pause. Everyone attendant upon* GODIVA'S *reply.*)

GODIVA. But, good Earl, how can I possibly ride through the market place of Coventry at high noon on

the bare back of that old horse when I'm stark naked?
I have hemorrhoids.

LEOFRIC.   Do they hurt?

GODIVA.   No; but they photograph dreadfully.

(LEOFRIC *removes a small tube from his left breast
pocket and gives it to* GODIVA.)

LEOFRIC.   Here, use this. In case of severe, prolonged
irritation, consult your physician. In case of death, dis-
continue use.

(GODIVA *screams and faints to the floor.* SUPERVIVA,
THOROLD *and* VERONICAS *rise simultaneously as she
falls.* THOROLD *rubs his hands with juicy anticipa-
tion.*)

THOROLD.   The High Noon Nude Ride of Lady Godiva
—Ah! a press agent's dream!!

LEOFRIC.   And now I must take my leave of this holy
convent. I shall return when it is time to fulfill my half
of the bargain. Adieu, O holy company.

(LEOFRIC *cracks his whip and disappears. The others
breathe more easy once he is gone.*)

VERONICAS.   Oh, my goodness, this whole thing has
been so dramatic: I don't know if I can bear the strain.

THOROLD.   You've *sustained* more than this in your
time, Veronicas, and you know it. This ain't nothin'.

SUPERVIVA.   Yeah, it's nowhere. They got hotter shows
every night at the Warwickshire Burlesque, and there
ain't such a long build-up before they take it off, either.

(TOM *comes out through the curtain with a quizzical
expression.*)

TOM.   Is this the Coventry Convent Infirmary?

VERONICAS (*sweetly*).   Yes, my good man, what can we
do for you?

TOM.   I have prickly heat.

(*They all laugh merrily and dance about in a
gavotte.*)

I'm a Yankee Doodle Dandy, and Yankee Doodles often
die. A real live nephew of my uncle lamb, scorned on
the troth of you lie!

VERONICAS.   You know, for a time there on the chaise,
I mean when they were really going at it, Lucky Pierre
had nothing *over* me. What was youse two doing?

SUPERVIVA. We was having Oepidus sex, sonny and me was.

VERONICAS *(firmly)*. Dinner is served!!

SUPERVIVA. That's my exit cue!

THOROLD. Mine, too. I'm fagged.

> (SUPERVIVA *and* THOROLD *bums rush each other out left.*)

VERONICAS. Tom, I'm starved. For affection, that is.

TOM. And all things thereto accruing. Sister, ya only gotta ask!

> (TOM *and* VERONICAS *go out left arm in arm. For a second the stage is silent and dim over the prostrate* GODIVA. *Then* TOM *returns immediately and comes far downstage.*)

Ladies and Gentlemen, this is the divertissement: it has nothing to do with the rest of the play, but then, divertissements seldom do. Actually, its purpose is to give the other actors time to change costumes. Basically, the divertissement is superficial—or superficially, it's basic.

> (TOM *clowns about briefly, his movements and manners very remindful of* GODIVA's *walk, gestures, movements and manners. Then he does a comic strip. His particulars remain undisclosed because he never removes the coin-exchange which dangles down over them. His efforts to remove his clothing without budging the coin-exchange should be as excruciating as they are funny. Then* TOM *goes upstage, permanently pulls aside one-half the sheer curtain, and mounts the horse, not as a taxi-driver this time, but rather imitating the traditional painting of Lady Godiva. He sits demurely and coyly on the horse, unless otherwise specified, from this point on until almost the end of the play.*
>
> SUPERVIVA, THOROLD, VERONICAS *and* LEOFRIC *re-enter left, dressed as angels. They are carrying onstage an enormous ladder: this ladder is wide enough to permit two persons to stand abreast on its rungs; also, it has rungs on both feet. They huff, puff and bicker, and finally set the ladder up in the center of the stage.* VERONICAS *has carried several stones onstage, which she places under* GODIVA's *head.*)

VERONICAS.   Take of the stones of this place, and put them for your pillows, sweetie.

(GODIVA *rises momentarily out of her faint to adjust to the awkward stones.*)

GODIVA.   Oh, —er—much obliged.

VERONICAS.   Forget it, sweetie, I get prop-man salary for that bit.

(GODIVA *falls promptly back into her faint. The others begin to mount the back foot of the ladder, one, two at a time. They caution each other to be very quiet during their ascensions, so as not to awaken* GODIVA. *When they reach the top of the ladder, they clumsily crawl over the top and begin descending the front foot. Then some go up and some go down, all with great difficulty, and, though they try to be serious and maintain angelic dignity, they constantly trip over each other's gowns, get in each other's ways, etc., and make a generally messy show of things. When a certain picturesqueness of position has been achieved, they all freeze and suddenly burst into deafening song.* GODIVA *awakes with a frightened start and beholds the vision before her.*)

ANGELS (*singing*).

> Behold, we are with thee!
> With thee, evermore!
> Where e'er thou goest
> We're with thee most.
> Where now thou liest
> There thou shalt diest.
> Hear, what's our need:
> Spread thou thy seed.
>
> Behold, we are with thee!
> With thee, evermore!
> Innermost and nethermost
> We are thy host.
> We'll bring thee back,
> So now hit the sack.
> We don't wanna boast—
> But we're with thee most!!

(*The* NUNS' CHORUS *is heard singing in the background in counterpoint to the above song.*)

CHORUS (*singing*).

> Morning horniness!
> O, what corniness!
> That's the thorniness—
> When you awake,
> For goodness' sake—
> Morning horniness!
> Morning horniness!

(*The following repartee between the* ANGELS *and* GODIVA *should be a very rapid exchange up until the revelation.*)

GODIVA. What are you all—a band of Thespians?

VERONICAS. Lespians, did she say?

SUPERVIVA. No, my child, the males among us are saints, the females, saintesses.

GODIVA. Oh, I see.

THOROLD. Shut up: we'll do the talking. You see nothing! First of all, be advised that spontaneous outbursts of joy are banned in public:—the reason being that the Earl might pass through at any given moment and needlessly suffer his sensibilities offense.

SUPERVIVA. Pleasure is also against the law. All unauthorized pin-up girls found sitting on street curbs will be summarily picked up!

LEOFRIC. Your father was a rapist!

VERONICAS. Your ma a swinging sadist!

SUPERVIVA. What will be in 30 years? I look at you, Godiva, and I think, "What will be in 30 years?" I mean, if you don't get married soon and spawn brats, how shall it be with you in 30 years? You know what I mean, you know exactly what I mean—how shall it be with me in 30 years?

VERONICAS. We're selling subscriptions. Want to subscribe, Godiva? There's the Saturday evening post, there's the N.Y. daily post . . . most expensive is the entire weekend post, under the lamplight.

LEOFRIC (*to* SUPERVIVA's *come-on*). Please, madam, one tittie at a time.

SUPERVIVA (*ignoring the snub*). You see, they used to think the bomb would solve everything. So everyone got lazy. But now they've forgotten how to make atomic bombs. All the taxes that used to go into military expenditures are currently being sunk into peace projects. So I repeat, what will be in 30 years?

LEOFRIC. Make up for lost time, but do not lose present time in the process!

> (SUPERVIVA *lights up another cigarette after being snubbed by* LEOFRIC. *Her cigarette holder gets in* THOROLD's *way.*)

THOROLD. Smoking again, Mother?

SUPERVIVA. Yes, Lord Raleighs. Ever notice he has balls instead of a beard?

THOROLD. Now listen carefully, Godiva: you are to be fairly forward with the angels, but within good taste, you understand? Sometimes you share a plaisanterie with them, sometimes you pinch their cheeks.

LEOFRIC. You can dye your hair in the rear.

SUPERVIVA. 30 years hath September, April, June and November. All the rest have 31 thousand millenniums, except February which doesn't have any days at all—and, child, it never will!!

THOROLD. I remember, I remember, Godiva, the house where we were born. And, believe me, I've done everything possible to forget it!

GODIVA (*despondent, confused*). I need a new nuance. Subtleties are O.K. in their place, but there's nothing like a nuance. A really new ance-er to everything.

SUPERVIVA. It is better to make use of everyday conceptions, and get double everything rolled into one.

VERONICAS. Some prefer cottontail candy.

LEOFRIC. And some a feminized dandy.

GODIVA (*impatient*). Listen, I ain't got all night! It's gonna be morning soon and I'll be waking up. Do or don't all you angels have some revelation to make?

SUPERVIVA. Yes, I do—I mean, we do. And hark me well, 'cause this is plot material! Good child, Godsend Godiva, sweet babe o' mine, I am your mother!

GODIVA. You are—?

SUPERVIVA. I repeat (*Belching.*) I am your mother.

GODIVA. My flesh and blood mother?

SUPERVIVA. Yes, my daughter, I am your flesh and blood mother. Rock-a-bye baby.

GODIVA.   How am I to accept that?

SUPERVIVA.   What's so hard to accept? Angelic revelations have contained much more shocking information—from time to time.

THOROLD.   And I, therefore, good Godiva, am your brother. Your flesh and blood brother.

GODIVA.   Well, that would follow logically.

LEFORIC.   Do not fret so, Godiva. Remember, an epiphany is just one god's opinion.

GODIVA.   True. But that won't save me from the pickle this one puts me in. According to this play, Thorold is my brother. And Mother Superviva *is* my real mother. Waking or dreaming, there's no wiggling out of that.

SUPERVIVA.   Ah, what a dutiful daughter! I knew she wouldn't deny her own mother. You see!

THOROLD.   Or her mother and brother's request that she ride nude through Coventry. Or would she?

LEOFRIC.   Well, Godiva, are you now willing to make your historic ride? Or do you have some legitimately defensible position from which to object to it?

GODIVA.   It's hard to say where I want to divide the legitimately defensible position from my neurosis—although these days who could divide the two?

SUPERVIVA.   My poor neurotic daughter! Hasn't your shrinker been of any help? Godivy, I do hope you're perfectly frank with your shrinker.

GODIVA *(shocked.)*   Really, Mother!—I try to keep our conversations on a high level at all times!

ANGELS *(singing)*.

> Godiva! Godiva! Godiva!
> Naughty nudie on a horse,
> Lovely limbed but slightly coarse,
> There's no warrant for remorse—
> We thy gallop strong endorse:
> So do what must be done
> And, doing so, have fun!

GODIVA.   I will, but what is it that really must be done?

ANGELS *(singing)*.

> Strip thyself of earthly dress:
> Topless gown we doubly bless:
> Angels at thy acquiesce
> Shalt thy nakedness caress!

> Then do what must be done
> And, doing so, have fun!

GODIVA. If God will be with me, and will keep me
in this ride that I go, and will give me hair to hide, and
raiment to put off, so that I come again to my mother's
house a piece; then shall the Lord be my God: And this
stone, which I have set for a pillar, shall be God's house:
and of all that she my mother shall give me I will surely
give the tenth unto Him.

VERONICAS. I take it she's gonna ride.

SUPERVIVA. Well, that's a weight off my chest!

ANGELS (*singing*).

> She'll ride! She'll ride!
> Hath thus decide
> For mother's hide!
> So dignified
> A horse bestride,
> If Leofric's lied,
> Then matricide—
> Godiva tried—
> Is justified!

GODIVA (*singing*).

> I'll ride! I'll ride!
> Though tits collide
> And legs divide,
> I'm purified—
> Or mother chide.

ANGELS, GODIVA, *and* CHORUS (*singing*).

> Then naked, naked ride
> Thou daughter mother's bride!
> For naught remains to hide:
> Betrothal now abide.

THOROLD. Well, that's over with!

LEOFRIC. And the name of this city called Luz at the
first, shall hereafter be called Death-el, Where She Rode,
Arizona.

VERONICAS. Wonder how Tom's making out?

(LEOFRIC *comes up behind* SUPERVIVA *on the ladder*

and pushes her falsies practically up to her neck.)

SUPERVIVA.   Oh! I'm up to my chin in troubles!

(*One of* SUPERVIVA's *falsies falls out onto the floor.*)

GODIVA.   You dropped a line, Mother.

LEOFRIC.   One could do worse than be a swinger of tits.

SUPERVIVA (*to* LEOFRIC).   Hey, could you change your rung?—you smell.

LEOFRIC.   Sorry, madam, just having some fun, that foreign word.

SUPERVIVA.   Well, go somewhere foreign and have it, if you don't mind! (*She pulls out the other falsie and casts it off, begins to descend the ladder toward* GODIVA.) I'm changing my channel, baby!!

> (*The* ANGELS *descend the ladder singing the last chorus, "Then naked, naked ride," over and again.* SUPERVIVA *advances menacingly toward* GODIVA, *divesting herself as she does, first of the angel's garb and, after that, of the nun's habit.* TOM *and* GODIVA *are both very frightened by this. Finally,* SUPERVIVA *stands revealed as a man. The others stop singing for a moment.*)

GODIVA.   Why, Mother, are you making overtures?

SUPERVIVA (*deep masculine voice*).   No, daughter, I'm going right into the first movement!

> (THOROLD, VERONICAS, LEOFRIC *and the* CHORUS *resume singing "Then naked, naked ride."* SUPERVIVA *seizes* GODIVA *and throws her to the floor.* TOM *falls to the floor by the horse in the self-same moment.* SUPERVIVA *falls on top of* GODIVA *and rapes her.* LEOFRIC *whips* VERONICAS *with his whip; she screams and rushes out left, still singing.* LEOFRIC *turns and whips* THOROLD.)

THOROLD.   Shit! I wish this were a different play—like Shakespeare or something!

LEOFRIC (*whipping him*).   Shakespeare?!—he belongs to the ages.

THOROLD (*in pain*).   Yeah—and this is one of them!

> (TOM *writhes on the floor by the horse as if being ravished.* VERONICAS *re-enters left carrying a dressing-screen which she places in front of the re-*

cumbent SUPERVIVA *and* GODIVA *to hide them from
the audience. But nothing hides* TOM*'s ignominy.*)

VERONICAS. Enough of the sordid details. Some people
have no modesty. We'll ban this scene to take the worry
out of being close.

THOROLD (*ducking the whip*). Kindly desist, I beg of
you, my noble earl! I don't think you realize just how
civil-minded I am!

LEOFRIC. Ha-ha! Don't you enjoy my kind of person?

THOROLD. Certainly—but you're the kind who's good in
well-spaced doses!

LEOFRIC (*holding up contraceptives*). Sale on contraceptives! Contraceptives for sale! Soiled! Second-hand!
Syphilitic! With holes punched in them!

(LEOFRIC *laughs demoniacally and tosses the contraceptives behind the dressing-screen. Then he cracks
his whip and whips* THOROLD *into lifting up the ladder and bearing it off stage-right.* LEOFRIC, *laughing evilly all the time, follows* THOROLD *out at right.*
VERONICAS *is excited by all the goings on and rushes
about the stage irrationally.*)

VERONICAS. Mississippi dyke attacked by waves! Watch
out for flying spumes! (*She spits at the audience.*)—
Spumes as many as the virginities that get lost at Niagara
Falls!! (*She is pensive for a second, points to the screen.*)
I'm supposed to cry throughout this whole scene . . .
dreadful scene, dreadful scene!

(VERONICAS *checks out the writhing* TOM, *spins
about, and slips out left. The singing of the* CHORUS
*lowers dramatically and slowly fades out. A second
of silence, and then* GODIVA *appears from behind
the dressing-screen. She is bedraggled, her dress
completely twisted, her hair-do all undone. She is
weeping.* TOM *rises, messy and worn, and remounts
the horse.*)

GODIVA. Ah, all these years and this long life spent
at nothing but an attempt to avoid that. That!—It was to
avert just that, that congress, to sidetrack *her*, that I
turned to prostitution! To love with all and thus love
none, no single one; to love not—*with her!* And how has
it profited me?

(GODIVA *and* TOM *dry their tears.* VERONICAS *comes bouncing back in nun's habit, carrying a wig long enough to hang down to the floor.* GODIVA *does not turn to face her.*)

VERONICAS. But you do love all, Lady Godiva, you do wish to demonstrate your love for all. That is why you will take this nude ride.

GODIVA. Will I?

VERONICAS. Won't you? To save the people? I mean, isn't that what you want to do, Godiva?

GODIVA. That vision of angels got me so mixed up, I almost thought I knew what I wanted. But it is nice to have known once what you were doing, and to no longer now . . .

(GODIVA *submits stoically while* VERONICAS *adjusts the long yellow wig over her head. It flutes stiffly against her back.*)

VERONICAS (*very satisfied*). A perfect fit—and so stylish, too! So arty-farty!

GODIVA. Where'd you commondear *this* rug? Wigs—how I hate them! They make you look ten years younger, and feel ten older.

VERONICAS (*stepping out of character into the actress that she really is*). I am the rug-maker's daughter! Don't laugh—just think whose daughter you are!

GODIVA (*stepping out of character into the actress that she really is*). For years the public has clammered to see more of me. This play answers their request!

(*At this point, the* NUNS' CHORUS *enters from behind the dressing-screen, a chorus line of Rockettes of sorts. They are each wearing a floor-length wig over their nun's habits. The wigs so completely cover them, only a single eye of each is visible; this somewhat impedes their attempts at graceful movement.* GODIVA *turns toward them in surprise.*)

CHORUS (*Brooklyn accents*). We hoid our cue.

GODIVA. What are they—male or female?

VERONICAS. If you can't tell, they ain't for you.

(*The striptease music starts and* GODIVA *and the* CHORUS *get in line ready to begin.* VERONICAS *stands aside watching.*)

TOM. Hum. Her mother must be real proud of her now.

  (GODIVA *sings, and talks where indicated, this bur-*
  lesque number, the CHORUS *dances in the back-*
  ground. GODIVA *strips slowly as she sings; when she*
  has finished her number, she is nude except for
  the long yellow draping wig.)

GODIVA (*singing*).
Welcome to Boston!
 Shoppin' for the brand of boy
 Partial to the type of toy
 That Mama wants to give him on his birthday . . .

I used to date those college guys
That had their heads up in the skies,
The kind that never used their eyes,
Forgot to zipper up their flies:

You gotta get your feet on earth—
Come down off that upper berth,
Believe me, College Joe, you'll find
A lot of worth in this girl's girth!

Hunters hanker after deer,
Go great lengths and know no fear,
But that healthy outdoor type
Never shot my home-cooked tripe.

Businessmen go ape for money,
Got no time to suckle honey,
Nothin's wrong with heaps of dough—
Except there are other heaps, you know:

CHORUS (*singing*).
    Like that extra pound
    So long as it's around
    That certain place
    —ain't ever outta place!

GODIVA. I mean, I used to wear these expensive off-the-shoulders type gowns: well, I been in a lot of parked cars in my day—and nobody ever nibbled on my shoulders!

   Then there is the muscle man
   Liftin' all the weights he can,

Workin' out in some hot gym—
Wastin' weights I've got for him.

Other fellas fancy poker,
Spend the night in smoky dens,
Leaving me at a loss to stoker
Up my fire with a poker.

What kind of a guy would I like to spend the evening
with in front of my fireplace?—oh, any really manly type—
like Rock Hudson, Rip Torn, Ed Fury, Chuck Steak or
Stark Naked.

Yeah, I'm shoppin' round and lookin'
For the fella likes home cookin',
For the boy who knows what's best:
Leg o' lamb, chicken breast.

Yeah, I've got a certain kind,
Special brand of boy in mind—
Just that homey type inclined,
Feelin' here and there, to find

CHORUS (*singing*).
That that extra pound
So long as it's around
That certain place
—ain't ever outta place!

GODIVA. And you better believe it:—I ain't the Singin'
Nun!

TOM. Well, well. She acquitted herself professionally.

VERONICAS. Will you be getting any money for your
ride, Lady Godiva?

GODIVA (*tough, resuming her Brooklyn accent at this
point*). No: I'm doing it for the exposure.

VERONICAS (*as in an Elizabethan play*). Soft you now:
here comes Thorold, the press agent.

(THOROLD *enters from the right; he is dressed as the
Sheriff once again, but with a press agent's hat on.*)

THOROLD. Ah! Lady Godiva:—she keeps a tired busi-
nessman awake. Hey! how come you got so much hair?

GODIVA. I'm retentive. Is that the nag I'm supposed
to ride? (*Indicating the wooden horse.*)

THOROLD. Yes. Its name is "Vehicle." A vehicle well suited to your burlesque charms.

GODIVA. "Vehicle," huh? Is it male or female?

THOROLD. Kneel, my child, and know.

GODIVA. Skip the religious bit:—I had this convent pegged for what it is from the start.

THOROLD. Why, Godiva, how could you speak so lightly of this establishment? Why, this is holy Coventry Convent.

GODIVA. More likely Coventry Convention, and not so holy. O.K., O.K., get the nag ready and let's get this show on the road.

THOROLD. Wait a minute, hold your horses:—I must announce you first. If you please, madam.

> (*Lights, a flourish, dramatic effects, the* CHORUS *quivering together,* VERONICAS *expectant,* GODIVA *very impatient.*)

Ladies and Gentlemen! Presenting for the first time on any stage and live before your startled eyes:—"The Life of Lady Godiva," a curtain raiser . . . A difficult subject, handled with delicacy and taste. And relish.

TOM. Hubba, hubba!

> (*A flourish, etc.,* GODIVA *moving whorishly toward the horse. Suddenly* SUPERVIVA *re-enters left on the arm of* LEOFRIC. *He is once again in his sado-masochist leather garb and is carrying his whip.* SUPERVIVA *is all done up like an opera Delilah. She carries a huge pair of shears. She and* LEOFRIC *are laughing like well-healed lovers. All movement stops and focuses on them.* SUPERVIVA *flexes the shears.*)

LEOFRIC. And then what happened?

SUPERVIVA *(laughing)*. Then when?

LEOFRIC. When you demanded of her that she go through with her historic ride.

> (SUPERVIVA *moves up to the* NUNS' CHORUS *as she speaks and begins cutting off their wigs, one by one, as if it were the most natural action in the world. The* CHORUS *line is too startled to defend itself adequately. Her physical masculine power overcomes each objector and her cries to desist.*)

SUPERVIVA. Well, it was very much like Greek tragedy,

you understand, what with the audience knowing the whole story in advance and all, and just sticking around to see *how* it would all come off, being all along well advised, of course, of *what* was coming off. It's all in the "how," not the "what." I.e., not the "what" am I, but the "how" am I, the "how I live." But then, you see, with Lady Godiva of Coventry, one of history's sexsational heroines, the Eternal Woman, etcetera, etcetera, etcetera, that need to have her personally love us, personally love me, shall never really be fulfilled. Clip, clip. Ah, yes, it is an imaginary perfection, however ardently sought, amongst our quotidian imperfections . . .

(*The* CHORUS *is scattered in outraged bewilderment. Their wigs, totally sheared, fall in heaps to the floor.* SUPERVIVA *surveys her work with satisfaction. Then she advances toward* GODIVA *with the awning shears extended menacingly.*)

GODIVA (*resuming her natural voice*). Who are you?

SUPERVIVA. I am Delilah—history's first female barber, and the Queen Bee of castration ladies.

GODIVA. I have submitted to you in everything. You turn your shears on me without provocation!

SUPERVIVA. Your cloaking, protective tresses are provocation enough, my child. Accept my apologies and kindly submit.

GODIVA. I do not like apologies. And I do not like the instances that necessitate them.

SUPERVIVA. Come, come, the morn shows the day, young harlot. You'll swim as well as Aquanetta soon as I've pared away your hindrances.

GODIVA. So—there are necrophiliacs in the tombs!

(GODIVA *steps back with unexpected quickness and wrests the whip out of* LEOFRIC's *hand. She holds off* SUPERVIVA, *threateningly. The others all freeze where they are.*)

SUPERVIVA. Who *are* you?

GODIVA. I am she who has policed her own ambitions, Mother. I am the corpse you had in mind.

SUPERVIVA. What an active cadaver! Leofric—protect me!

LEOFRIC. I beg your pardon?

SUPERVIVA. I said protect me, defend me from that monster!

GODIVA. Of your filial making!

LEOFRIC. What did you say, Delilah?

SUPERVIVA. Don't you speak British, Earl Leofric, don't you understand me? (*Very frightened, rushing from one to the other.*) Thorold, you, my son, help me!!

THOROLD. What did you say, Delilah?

SUPERVIVA. Can't you comprehend me, either?

THOROLD. No, I can't. But I think you're repeating (*Belching.*) yourself.

SUPERVIVA. Sister Veronicas, Leofric—

LEOFRIC. Please, Superviva, words are an art form. Stop trying to use them to communicate with.

SUPERVIVA (*desperate*). Thorold! what should I do?

THOROLD. Look demure and coy, such is always effective when there are no appropriate stage directions.

VERONICAS. Or try snubbing everyone. That usually goes over in a pinch.

SUPERVIVA (*frantic, with* GODIVA *advancing on her*). Will nobody rescue me? I, who am the mother of all? Don't I get out of this tight spot?

LEOFRIC. I'm afraid you don't.

SUPERVIVA. That's funny: my friends never seem to read the same history books I do.

> (GODIVA *cracks the whip and knocks the shears from out of* SUPERVIVA'S *hand.* SUPERVIVA *trembles in dread.*)

GODIVA. Your poetry is minor, Mother, your hang-ups major! All products to the test of market now!

SUPERVIVA. But, Godiva, think about tomorrow!!

GODIVA. Why should I? Tomorrow never thought about me!

SUPERVIVA. You idiots, you ungrateful bastards, all of you! World War Three will teach you all a lesson . . .

> (GODIVA *whips* SUPERVIVA *and pushes her down to the floor on her hands and knees. The others do not move.*)

GODIVA. In dreams the stopped blood of February has already begun mulling over the changing fashions of madness . . . Tally-ho! (GODIVA *cracks the whip again and mounts* SUPERVIVA's *back as if she were a horse.*)

SUPERVIVA. Godiva, think of what you're doing, think of the commitment you're making! You may have to live the rest of your life like this!

GODIVA. Mother, you may have to live the rest of your life.

SUPERVIVA (*crying*). Godiva, my child, my darling daughter, have you no mercy for she who gave you birth? You are my flesh and blood daughter!

GODIVA. What do you mean your daughter? Have you ever seen me for the thing I was, stood to the side of the thing I am? What am I ever but a dream of you, fantasy versions of your own self, your projects down-decade projected and utterly minimized? I am fenced in the claustrophobic saddle of your back, like the whole wide world on the shell of a tortoise—you have never provided another place in your imagination for me to exist.

(*A flourish.* THOROLD *rushes up to* GODIVA *and gives her a riding stick.*)

THOROLD. Presenting Lady Godiva of Leicestershire, Warwickshire, Worchestershire and Newark—New Jersey! Lady Godiva rides nude at high noon! Turn up the lights, will you? Full house lights on for high noon—let nothing, not a single detail be hidden!

(*The stage lights go up to their full brilliance.* GODIVA *stabs* SUPERVIVA's *side with the riding stick and begins to prod her into moving off as if she were a horse.*)

LEOFRIC. Godiva atop her named terrors, and by this act becomes she an adult.

(TOM, *with his special Peeping-Tom prongs and instruments, pries aside the sheer curtain and peers at the riding* GODIVA.)

TOM (*in Mexican accent*). Hubba, hubba!

LEOFRIC. Who are you?

TOM. I am Tom, the Peeping Tom. *The* Peeping Tom of history, if you please. A voyeur, to you.

LEOFRIC. What does that mean?

TOM (*peering through a telescope*). Voyeurism?—Oh, it's a sitting back and watching proposition. A watching of yourself.

LEOFRIC. But you're playing the Peeping Tom on Lady Godiva.

TOM. So? If I'm watching her, she and I are the same person really. Ay! hubba, hubba! I mean, aren't we? I mean—that's me out there on the horse and I'm back here by the horse, not responsible at all, you see, but responsible of all, you see, an audience, a Godiva, of sorts.

VERONICAS (*cobbling the shoes*). He don't make horse-sense.

THOROLD. Forget him, Leofric, he's just a brutish, imbecilic cabbie.

TOM. Hey, Leofric, how does this plot wind up, anyhow?

LEOFRIC. It winds up tragically. Despite her naked ride through Coventry at high noon, I never remit the tax.

THOROLD. You don't? A bit of leather, aren't you, Earl Leofric? S-M at the fringes.

TOM. Bastard!

> (*At this point, the end of "Les Préludes" begins to play. The* NUNS' CHORUS *re-enters slowly from the left and slowly moves toward the right. There is something suggestive of riding movement in their steps.* VERONICAS, *frantically cobbling the soles of the shoes, at last completes her work. She rushes up to* GODIVA *and fits them on her bare feet.*)

VERONICAS. Lady Godiva, my martyred child, your oxfords are finally fixed. There, dear, that's it,—so you won't be completely naked!

GODIVA (*sadly*). Thank you, Sister Veronicas. The only article I don't need, since I'm riding. Someday, have faith, Sister Veronicas, and pornography will be accepted. (*Smiling slightly.*) But nudity shall never be understood.

> ("*Les Préludes" whelms up to a full blast.*)

Giddyup! Giddyup!

> (GODIVA *rides* SUPERVIVA *out right with the* NUNS' CHORUS *following;* TOM *peeping with delight.*
> *Curtain.*)

BIBLIOGRAPHY

Other works by the playwrights represented in this volume:

GRANT DUAY
Fruit Salad is Grant Duay's first play.

MARIA IRENE FORNES
The Widow (produced at Casa del las Americas, Cuba, then in the Actors Studio workshop, New York City).
The Wise Parrot (winner of an honorable mention in a play-writing contest at Stanford University; unproduced).
There! You Died (produced at the Blau-Irving San Francisco Actors' Workshop, and later at the Spoleto Festival of Two Worlds in Italy. Subsequent productions at East End Theatre and at IASTA in New York City).
Tango Palace (a revised version of *There! You Died.* Produced at Actors Workshop, New York City, and at Firehouse Theatre, Minneapolis. Published in *Playwrights for Tomorrow*, University of Minnesota Press).
The Office (produced at Actors Studio Workshop, New York City, and later revised for Broadway presentation under the direction of Jerome Robbins. This production closed during previews prior to a formal "opening").
The Successful Life of 3 (produced at The Open Theatre, New York City, and revived at the Judson Church, New York. Published in *Eight Plays from Off-Off Broadway*, Bobbs-Merrill, and in *Playwrights for Tomorrow*, University of Minnesota Press).
A Vietnamese Wedding (produced at Judson Memorial Church, New York City).

MURRAY MEDNICK
    The Box (produced at Theatre Genesis, New York City).
    The Mark of Zorro (produced at Theatre Genesis, New York City, as a mixed-media presentation, with film by Harold Aranoff).
    Guide Line (produced at Theatre Genesis, New York City).

ROCHELLE OWENS
    Futz (Living Theatre on European tour. Later produced by the La Mama Experimental Theatre Club, New York City. Published in *New American Plays,* Vol. II, Hill & Wang).
    The String Game (produced by Judson Poets' Theatre, New York City).
    Homo (produced by the La Mama Experimental Theatre Club, New York City, for its first European tour).
    Beclch (produced by The Theatre of the Living Arts, Philadelphia).

TOM SANKEY
    The Teacher (produced at New York University).
    The Frammis (unproduced).
    The False Premise (showcase production in New York City).
    My Daddy Is Dying (produced by Theatre Genesis in New York City).
    25 Year Dialogue (unproduced).
    Green Bray (unproduced).

SAM SHEPARD
    Cowboys (produced at Theatre Genesis, New York City).
    Rock Garden (produced at Theatre Genesis, New York City).
    Up to Thursday (produced by the Barr-Wilder-Albee experimental theatre, New York City).
    4-H Club (produced by the Barr-Wilder-Albee experimental theatre, New York City).
    Dog (produced at La Mama Experimental Theatre Club, New York City).

Rocking Chair (produced at La Mama Experimental Theatre Club, New York City).

Icarus' Mother (produced at Caffe Cino, New York City, and the Theatre Company of Boston).

Fourteen Hundred Thousand (produced at the Firehouse Theatre of Minneapolis, WNDT television, New York City, and national NET TV).

Chicago (produced at Theatre Genesis, New York City, and the La Mama Experimental Theatre Club for presentation in New York and in Europe, published in *Eight Plays from Off-Off Broadway,* Bobbs-Merrill).

La Turista (produced at the American Place Theatre, New York City).

RONALD TAVEL

Christina's World (published in *The Chicago Review,* 1963, unproduced).

Screen Test (produced by Theatre of the Ridiculous, New York City, and later at Queens College and Columbia University. Filmed by Andy Warhol).

Tarzan of the Flicks (produced at Goddard College).

The Life of Juanita Castro (published in *Tri-Quarterly* (1966), and produced at Coda Galleries and moved to St. Marks Playhouse, New York City. Later performed at Rutgers University, and revived by Theatre of the Ridiculous. Performed also at Northwestern University. Filmed by Andy Warhol).

Shower (produced at Coda Galleries, and moved to St. Marks Playhouse, both in New York City).

Vinyl (unproduced, but filmed by Andy Warhol, 1967).

Kitchenette (published in *Partisan Review.* Produced by Theatre of the Ridiculous and by Coda Galleries in New York City. Also performed in New York's St. Marks Playhouse. Filmed under the title *Kitchen* by Andy Warhol).

Indira Gandhi's Daring Device (produced by Theatre of the Ridiculous, and later at Rutgers University and Columbia University).

Gorilla Queen (produced at Judson Church, New York City, and off-Broadway at the Martinique Theatre in New York).

JEAN-CLAUDE VAN ITALLIE

Pavane (initially produced by La Mama Experimental Theatre Club, New York City, and later incorporated into the triple bill bearing the overall title *America Hurrah* as a part of an expanded one-act play re-titled *Interview*).

America Hurrah (initially produced at La Mama Experimental Theatre Club, New York City, and later incorporated into the triple bill bearing the overall title *America Hurrah* as the playlet *Motel*. Published in *Eight Plays from Off-Off Broadway*, Bobbs-Merrill, under its original title).

TV (a one-act play comprising the third play in the triple bill bearing the overall title *America Hurrah* and played off-Broadway at the Pocket Theatre in New York City).

War (initially produced at the Village South Theatre, New York, and then at the Caffe Cino, New York City).

Dreams (initially produced at the La Mama Experimental Theatre Club, New York City, and later presented as a part of *6 from La Mama* at the Martinique Theatre, New York).

It's Almost Like Being (published in the *Tulane Drama Review*, 1963; unproduced except in The Open Theatre workshop in New York City).

Hobbies; or Things Are All Right with the Forbushers (television play commissioned by CBS for presentation on *Look Up and Live* in 1967).